LECTURES

ON THE

WORKS AND GENIUS

OF

WASHINGTON ALLSTON.

BY

WILLIAM WARE,

AUTHOR OF

ZENOBIA, AURELIAN, JULIAN, &c.

BOSTON:
PHILLIPS, SAMPSON AND COMPANY.
M DCCC LII.

THURSTON, TORRY, AND EMERSON, PRINTERS.

EDITOR'S PREFACE.

The Lectures contained in this volume are given to the public, as they were left by the author, at his death. There might, perhaps, be some question as to the propriety of giving to the world an unfinished work of criticism upon such a subject; but the words of the author himself, in speaking of the great unfinished picture of the Artist, whose name and fame it was his object, so far as it was in his power, to make more extensively known and honored among us, furnish a sufficient apology. It seems to be, "a work from which lessons may be drawn of use to society; too valuable, too beautiful, too much of it near its completion, too instructive, in many ways, to be rolled up forever, or seen by a few and hidden from the common eye."

The preparation of these Lectures was a work of love; the opinions expressed, the result of a long and loving study of the subject; and, though it may be that, before publication, they would have undergone some modification from his own hand, which that of another cannot venture to undertake, it is believed that they are mainly the result of careful study and deliberate conviction.

The author, at the time he was suddenly attacked by his last illness, was engaged in making arrangements for delivering these Lectures in this city, so long the residence of the illustrious Artist and Scholar of whose works and genius they treat. To the last sentence, which is here given as it was left unfinished by his pen, it was the author's intention to add a conclusion adapted to the circumstances of the place, and to the audience to whom it would have been first addressed.

CAMBRIDGE, Massachusetts, August, 1852.

THE CHARACTERISTICS OF ALLSTON'S GENIUS.

CONTENTS.

THE CHARACTERISTICS OF ALLSTON'S GENIUS.

In the Lectures which I propose to read upon Mr. Allston and his works, upon his works, rather than upon him, (upon him, only incidentally,) it will be my object to present some account of them; in order to increase and extend, if it may be, what I cannot but regard as just impressions of their value and importance, to artists, to all lovers of art, and to the cultivated portion of society at large.

But, really, it seems idle to think of reading Lectures upon such a subject, so far off and dead, while our public is all alive with Liberty, Intervention, Hungary and Russia, French Revolution, and a thousand other topics no less engrossing; — it seems much as if one were to propose a course upon the virtues and duties of moderate exercise, while one's city was burning down. I can look for but a few hearers under such circumstances, and a few will satisfy my wishes.

I shall go, somewhat minutely, into criticisms of these works. Some may think this not very well judged, as but few, it may be thought, can be supposed to have seen them, and but few, therefore, are able to form any opinion on what may be offered. But I believe that the having seen them, or not, would make but little difference in an easy understanding or enjoyment of the subject, to any who would enjoy such a subject at all. It were better, no doubt, on the whole, were the memory familiar with the works to be named; but it can, by no means, be necessary. Hardly more so than it would be, in the reading of literary criticism, that all the books criticised should first have been read, which would be better, but not essential to the receiving a great deal of pleasure and instruction. Suppose some La Harpe, Sismondi, Tiraboschi, were to offer a course of lectures upon the History of English Literature, how very few could attend such a course, and how much pleasure and information would be lost, were it to be confined to those only who had read all the volumes that were to form the subject-matter of the course.

For my own part, I listen to criticisms on pictures, and the works of famous artists, in their biographies, or in lectures, with as much interest, and enter into them as heartily, as to criticisms on any subjects purely literary. Descriptions, I can follow as readily as analyses of dramas, poems, novels, histories; as well as details of campaigns, battles, sieges, and can come to as intelligent an opinion. And this, without any thing more being requisite than attention; with no necessity whatever for any particular acquaintance with, or knowledge of, any of the purely mechanical departments of the art. In fact, all the more important statements and criticisms in relation to art, have a closer relation to what is universal in its character, common alike to literature and art, than to any thing peculiar and restricted. And particularly is this true when criticisms relate to a mind so universal in its tastes and attainments as that of Mr. Allston. With this explanation, I shall feel myself as fully justified in any minuteness of detail in my subject, as I should, in the case of an exclusively literary topic. Yet shall I be none the less anxious to avoid the too much and the too minute. I shall hope not to make my subject tedious, though I naturally experience some apprehensions.

Before I proceed to the particular enumeration of Mr. Allston's characteristics as an artist, I wish to glance at some of the foundations and reasons of his eminence and success.

In the first place, Mr. Allston was prepared for a successful career by his general cultivation. This should be well considered by the young aspirant. It had much to do in his case, and always, in any case, must have much to do, with success. I do not enter into the question of his natural genius, how great it was, as a reason and explanation of his eminence ; nor, to what extent his fame was owing to genius, rather than to his culture of it. We never can know or tell how much God has originally given, nor how much withheld. All that we can affirm, in any case, with certainty is, whether any thing, and if any thing, how much, man has done. If much, it will be fair and right to ascribe to culture much of the grand total of success. If absolutely nothing, or but little, then the eminence, if manifested, will be, as justly, ascribed to God, or to genius. But I can call to mind scarce an instance of a transcendently great artist, who was great, independently of labor, and great labor. In literature, Shakspeare comes nearer than any other human being, to the case of pure, exclusive genius. We have no evidence that he ever was a scholar or student, that he ever did any thing save merely to transcribe the ideas that crowded upon his mind ; only, that he is known to have hunted through volumes of old novels, histories and translations, for the themes of his plots. Homer, on the other hand, the other great genius of the world, as he began life as a schoolmaster, may, with reason, be supposed to have been a man of work, more or less, — most likely more. Not at all, that I am inclined to deny or underrate genius, in comparison with labor, in art. I believe that in art, as in literature, there is the greatest inequality conceivable in the human powers. I would as soon believe that all men and women are born equally handsome, well-shaped, or strong, as that they are created equal in intellectual power; — as soon believe that the ugly may be made beautiful by washes and unguents, the crooked, straight, by mechanical appliances, as that any efforts of labor can ever supply a natural intellectual deficiency. But I think that, generally, they who have been preëminently indebted to nature for their superiority, are they, who have added as much as ever nature did for them, by their own efforts. Particularly was that so with those intellectual giants, Da Vinci, Michael Angelo, and Raffaelle. Without their unremitting, herculean labors, what would they have been, with all their genius? In all the instances of Allston's peculiar success, we cannot conceive of that success being attained without all of that application by which he was distinguished. And really, without such application, no one knows what his genius is, nor how great. Claude was a remarkable instance of this. In color, which was Allston's grand distinction, though feeling, or genius, was its foundation, the most pains-taking labors could alone have raised the superstructure.

In the first suggestion of his subjects and their management, how much must he not have been indebted to his general cultivation of mind! How much must it not have added to the general dignity of his character, and imparted the vigor, grace and elegance of learning, to his design! No one can look upon the works that come from his hand, without perceiving, at a glance, his indebtedness to the highest intellectual culture; in the same way as one would, from reading such poetry as Bryant's, or such prose as Irving's.

Another explanation of Allston's eminence, was the truthfulness and earnestness of his mind, its simplicity and unselfishness, the noble and elevated principles on which he acted and pursued his art. He made pictures, not, that they might be sold and enrich him ; not, that they might bring him reputation now, and fame afterwards ; not, that he might eclipse others, and throw them into the shade ; from that he shrunk with instinctive horror ; but, because he loved and honored his art on its own account ; because, through it, as a medium, he could express himself in the best way possible to him ; because, in this manner only, could he reveal to others his conceptions of the beautiful, the grand, the divine. He certainly had a proper regard for the prices which his works would bring ; he was to live by his art ; and he demanded the full sum which he thought they were worth, as a matter of just self-respect, but he made no demand till he had made the very picture which he wished to make, and as he wished to make it. He loved reputation ; but would seek or accept it, only as the fair reward of labors honestly and entirely his own, both in the conception and the execution, and completed up to the highest mark of his ability. In regard to the particular subject of any picture, he chose it, not, for any reason of momentary popularity, or, because it would sell well, or exhibit well, nor at the urgency of others, nor for any idle whim or fancy ; but because he himself had fallen in love with it, and he could not rest till it was done ; his imagination was inflamed, and the fire spread and communicated power to his whole being. He then was in a condition to work, and he worked, as a man, then only, does. When a man paints a picture, or does any kind of work, on such principles, he works well. He paints, sculptures, writes well. A book, poem, novel, history, written in such a way, stands a chance of being read longer than while the ink is drying. To draw an illustration from my own profession, sermons written in this way only, are good ones. An eminent sermonizer of our own time, I have heard say, that he would not begin to write a sermon, let what would happen, till he knew what to write about (what a censure on most of us!) nor only that, not till he had found something that he wanted to say, and believed he knew how to say. And he waited often, weeks and weeks, before he could move. But, when the work was done, it *was* done; the man was in the sermon; and whatever there was in him of intellectual or moral power, these passed over to the hearer and possessed him; it was so, so only, that Allston undertook his pictures. They are, in no instance, painted without the deepest meditation and the profoundest study. This is obvious to any one who knows any thing about them. He has, in each case, found a thought which he wished to utter, which he was burning to utter, into which, then, by degrees and by prolonged study, he concentrated every faculty, affection, knowledge of his mind. Then he painted; and to say that he succeeded, is only to proclaim a natural, irresistible effect, of the means and methods employed.

This, undoubtedly, was the principal reason, why, comparatively, and, for a person of his power, he painted so few pictures. He could not paint many done in that way. A man so thoroughly conscientious, who made a conscience of his art, could not make many; too many conditions were to be satisfied for that. Had he been willing to paint pictures on the principles on which so many make them, men, too, who have been eminent in their profession, he might easily have rolled in wealth, instead of dying, as he did, in a more honorable poverty. But whether, in that way, his reputation would have gained, is another thing.

Mr. Allston's mind was a religious mind — another reason of his success. He looked at subjects, as he looked at nature, through a religious medium. Every thing was colored by it to his eye. This was a great happiness to him, as a man, as it was a great additional source of power, as an artist. Beato Angelico was not more a religious man than he — nor Overbeck; religious in no one-sided, technical sense, but in the universal sense. He was, indeed, of a particular church ; but he was, in religion, what he so emphatically declared himself in art, a wide liker ; by charity in religion, and benevolence in art, he was alike distinguished. It is delightful once more to see religion in so close alliance with art. If an undevout astronomer is mad, what shall be said of the artist ? One would think it could hardly be otherwise, than that the student of nature, for the simple, beautiful ends of art, should be religious, in the sense of a devotional mind ; penetrated with sentiments of reverence and love, for the grandeur and the loveliness of the Creator's works. Were it oftener so, it is easy to see what a spirit of elevation it would necessarily communicate to art, to what a different class of subjects it would lead the mind, to what a different manner of treating them ; in a word, into how different, and more exalted a state it would bring it, and from how much loftier a point it would view all subjects that came within its sphere. It will not necessarily declare itself by the selection and treatment of subjects distinctively religious. By no means. Though it will naturally do this, occasionally. It will rather, reveal itself indirectly, but only the more powerfully. And here, one cannot but sometimes regret, and yet, with misgivings, that, while Allston was so eminently of a religious spirit, it should not, oftener, have drawn him away from his devotion to the purely beautiful; that it should never, in a single instance, have led him for his theme, to the New Testament. But I am inclined to think that it was his religious reverence that deterred him — no indifference; that scriptural subjects, the only ones that would prove attractive to him, which another might treat, with no doubt as to their fitness and propriety, he could not touch, at all, or without trembling; without trembling too much to command a free use of his powers, or even think it right to use them so at all. This is but a conjecture, but plausible, as it seems to me.

Since writing this as a conjecture, I have been happy to find the conjecture verified in a brief article written by Dr. Channing at the time of Mr. Allston's death, to whom he distinctly declared, that "He never could make that person, or those characters, Christ and his Apostles, subjects of his art."

Another foundation of his eminence was, that he so often painted upon a large scale, the scale of life, or colossal, that it led to the formation, not only of a correct, but an elevated hand, to the avoiding of all that class of faults, and all that sort of looseness and littleness of manner, the attendant and result of confinement to diminutive forms, and pictures of cabinet size. The schools do wisely, when the absolute requisition is made of the pupil, that every drawing shall be made of the size of life, or, otherwise, collossal. It leads, with certainty, to correctness and truth of form, and gradually, to a grand style of drawing, and even higher style of thinking and designing. It elevates the mind as well as improves the hand. On the other hand, beneath drawings on a diminutive scale, are safely hidden away a thousand inaccuracies and errors, which the observer cannot distinguish nor detect to be such. It is impossible to judge, in such a case, whether the work of an artist be correct or not. The very power to judge is taken away. In reply to this, it would be a mere sophism to maintain that, because the drawing of the human form should be of the size of life, or more, houses and trees should be as well, to be judged true. All that is meant is, that all objects shall be of such a size, that the eye shall be easily capable to make such comparisons with reality, as to be able to discriminate between what is correct and incorrect; which cannot be done when the scale is miniature. Accustomed to the large scale, the eye, at once, detects the faulty, in one's own work, or in another's. But, much more than this, it elevates the general style of art, impresses upon it, more than any other cause, I believe, that grand manner, as it is termed, in the way of thinking and drawing, which gave its sublime character to the era of the fifteenth and sixteenth centuries.

And, to my mind, one of the prominent causes of the decline of art at the close of those centuries, was the fall of the Catholic Church; for, with that church disappeared the broad field for the exercise of art, on that scale essential to its grandeur. During the centuries just named, fresco was the kind of art universally employed. The vast panels for that art were furnished by nothing less than the walls and ceilings of churches and cathedrals. The colossal was the scale employed; this, of itself, was enough to stamp a character of grandeur upon art. The intellectual and mechanical advantage derived from that sweep of the arm which designing on so vast a scale, imparts, can hardly be enough appreciated. Add to this, that, as far as the church was concerned, it was religion that alone supplied the subjects for the pencil, and no other cause can be needed to account for the elevation to which painting was raised at that time. The rise and predominance of Protestantism, while it gave new life to Religion, struck Art with a palsy, from which it seems as if it could never recover, nor, perhaps, ever will, till some new Church shall arise, which, bent on truth, not on party, shall not be afraid to revive all that was good, beautiful in the elder church, while it still prosecutes its work of reform. Ages often drop, and leave forgotten behind, treasures as choice as any new ones they may find on the road, or invent, as they go along. Such effects as these named have not universally followed, of course, nor has art universally declined, but that it has suffered very materially, none can doubt. Allston's paintings of the human form, with but few exceptions, were of the size of life, or larger. This was one cause of his excellence.

Another cause of his success, which I may name, was the conscientious exactness with which he finished, to the utmost of his ability, every work which he undertook. The labor, toil, finish of art could go no further than in the case of this brilliant artist, who was never so solicitous to achieve a great work, or extend his reputation, or to gather laurels, as he was to finish, with almost Dutch minuteness, whatever labor he had commenced and promised.

I turn, now, to some of the characteristics of Mr. Allston's art. I shall take up these points: Mr. Allston's color; his appreciation of character, or power of expression; his love of beauty; and his feeling for the sublime; but with no severe strictness of method.

The grand, distinguishing characteristic of Mr. Allston, as an artist, that which, at once, raises him, not only above our own artists, but I am equally clear, above all others, certainly of the present day, is *Color*. He was great in many ways, but greatest there; for one, I am ready to say, unapproached. And, it is to be observed, that, to excel in color, is to excel in by no means an inferior department of art. Excepting only, in the purely intellectual power of the conception and composition of those grand designs which express the greatest thoughts of genius, and which have filled the world with works that can never die, which have lived for ages, and will live for ages to come, in the admiration of successive generations — Color, in its perfection, more than any thing else, proves an original mind, proclaims that gift of nature which we describe by the word genius; an excellence to be acquired by no labor, no art, no teaching, by no processes of reason, by no search after principles. None can teach it to another; none can learn it from another. It is a feeling, an instinct, a heaven-given, heaven-born virtue; a thing that God gives, which man cannot otherwise possess. It may be approximated, more or less remotely, by effort, study, and imitation, but not reached. We call it appropriately, genius; it is nothing else. More strictly, is this great excellence of color, thus denominated, than even the power I first named, invention and composition. If, to a knowledge and skill in form, be added the highest intellectual culture, in a mind of great natural vigor, one can easily suppose that the mind of an artist may be so far exalted, that he shall be able to conceive and express subjects the most subtle and the most complex, with that perfection, that both the requisitions of logic and of the imagination shall be fully satisfied. But, on the other hand, as to the feeling, by which the brush shall be arrested, at the point when absolute truth and absolute beauty shall be reached, in the color of a head, the tint of a sky, or the gradations of a distance ; this is native in the soul, and, like the perception of color itself, is a grace beyond the art of teaching or learning. Unless schools and masters can work miracles, they can do nothing. I say they are powerless to reach perfection. To borrow an illustration from a kindred department, color, is to painting, what the choice of words is, to style, in literature. The highest graces of style, as every body knows, are beyond the reach of professors, and cannot be imparted by them, even though they be models themselves. Errors can be corrected and faults amended, to any extent, but beauty, grace, cannot be imparted, any more than beauty and grace of movement can be imparted, by the dancing-master, to the body which nature has constructed awkwardly. All the wisdom and genius of Universities, cannot make a single

Addison or Goldsmith or Irving out of a raw material designed by Heaven for something very different. In truth, the more style is taught by laborious processes, the further, I believe, it flees from the love-sick votary. It is an impalpable essence, that eludes, like some airy phantom, the grasp of him who attempts to seize it. Imitators may herd around a great man who has originated a transcendent excellence; and imitation will produce resemblance, but nothing more, — no real excellence; and a far inferior grace, if original, is worth it all. A copyist is he who must be considered as, least of all, hopeful of any good and lasting success. The color of Palma, Correggio, Titian, cannot be taught or learned. Titian was surrounded by scholars, yet not one of them equalled Titian. To himself and his pupils, there were common, the same pigments, the same vehicles, the same tools and other mechanical contrivances. They might stand by and watch the miraculous hand as it laid on the tints; but it all availed not, till the genius to use the tools and the methods could be imparted as well; in short, till one mind could be inserted into another. I do not believe that a single process was concealed from those whom he professed to teach. I believe that he freely imparted all the artifices or tricks of color, which he himself practised or knew. And, if pupils were, in any case, as I have seen affirmed by some writers, not permitted to overlook him at work, a much more probable explanation of the fact may be found in the unwillingness which any one who has secured a great reputation, will naturally feel, to admit witnesses of the blunders, mistakes, changes, and alterations, through which he is seen to work his difficult way to what, at last, seems so perfect, and which he would rather have believed to have leaped from the brain at once, full armed, in all its panoply of beauty and glory. Such changes seem a confession of infirmity; erroneously, but naturally enough.

In the same way, Allston made no secret of his art. He was no quack, dealing with hidden nostrums. He was ever ready to impart to any who sought him, the materials he used, and to describe the order and succession of his tints, and all the various other processes by which he produced his wonderful results. But on whom has the mantle of his genius fallen? Some few learned so far as to catch some of his more obvious peculiarities; but, of his unrivalled carnations, no one, I believe, ever attempted an imitation. Any one must see that it is the native eye, the heaven-descended feeling for color, which makes the consummate artist; that this is a mental attribute, and lies, not in the cunning hand, alone; and that, in truth, the hand has cunning only because the mind has it first.

This original genius for color was eminently Titian's, Correggio's, Allston's. I am not afraid to place those names in immediate juxtaposition, though Allston himself might have shrunk from the distinction. If any one will compare the coloring of Allston with that of Titian, he will perceive that, while the results are different, so as to prove a proper independence of one over the other, the one is not inferior to the other. I am ready to say this deliberately, and with my most entire conviction of its unexaggerated truth. I may be mistaken, of course, but such is my opinion. And this obliges me to add, that I cannot, willingly, yield to many, a power of discrimination in respect to truth of color. When I knew, a few years ago, that I was about to have an opportunity to see the works of *Titian*, I examined, with renewed attention, all the best examples of Allston ; and when, after a careful study of very many of the best instances of Titian's pencil, I returned, and, with that experience fresh in my mind, again reëxamined the best works of Allston, I felt that, in the great Venetian, I had found nothing more true, nothing more beautiful, nothing more perfect, than I had already seen in Allston. I cannot but think that most persons, who should go through the same process, would arrive at the same result. When I passed from the Venus to the Valentine, I could acknowledge no falling off. The hues of the one were no less perfect than those of the other. It was nature in both, and nature when most beautiful.

They both sought to represent nature when adorned, and adorned the most. There was no Tuscan nor Doric, in their style; it was more even than Corinthian. Nor was their taste ever at fault, though they so preferred, and practised, the gorgeous. Their hues never glare upon the eye. All the deepest and richest tints are there, but in such harmonious union, that a divine simplicity seems the only result. Just as in nature, we know, it is a complexity which baffles all comprehensions, by which every hue is produced which gives enchantment to a landscape, to the color of a cheek or a hand. In the case of such artists, their colors are so broken, and mingled, and contrasted, that no one tint ever predominates and stares upon the eye; art is concealed and buried beneath nature.

But it need hardly be said that Allston was not always, equally felicitous, even in color, where he most excelled. This should be remembered by all who would judge or criticise him. It is only right and fair that the opinion should be formed of him, of what he was, and of what he could do, by the finest examples of his power. Sometimes, he seemed, for a while, to have lost the delicacy of his eye and truth of his feeling, as well as the cunning of his hand; as, for instance, in that picture called the Amy Robsart. But this cannot be accounted strange or unusual. The same occasional inferiority of hand is to be noted in Titian, Correggio; many a picture by those masters could hardly be determined, by evidence alone, to be the work of their pencil. But much the greater part of all that came from Allston's hand, whether history, ideal portrait, landscape, or still life, is sufficiently marked by his felicitous and peculiar touch and color, to show the same mastery over nature, and reveal the same inimitable beauties. The most perfect examples of Allsston's color may be found, I think, in the Jeremiah and the Valentine, in the Spanish Girl, and in portions of the Belshazzar. There are many others which are little inferior to these. I single out these; the first, for the most perfect example of flesh color, and the Jeremiah for the variety of color manifested, and for the perfection with which such a variety of tints is managed, for producing a unity of effect beyond any thing that could be well imagined; a harmony, rich and delicious like the Fifth Symphony of Beethoven, — or one of nature's sunsets, when all her infinite pallette is employed, with all her inexhaustible resources.

I have just mentioned that there may be the greatest inequality in the color of a great colorist. The reason for it is found in the very definition given of this process, as, in its perfection, being the result of feeling or genius, rather than the result, even of the most scientific and careful education. Genius is proverbially unequal. The work which is the result of feeling, not science, cannot but be so. The fortunate execution which was yesterday's achievement, cannot, with any certainty, be repeated to-day; the drawing may be, but not the color. That execution was good fortune, it was nothing that can be done again with absolute certainty of the same result. The results of genius must always possess this uncertainty. Talent, on the other hand, which works under the guidance of accurate knowledge and settled principles, moves in one and the same direction, and accomplishes, with little error, the same foreseen, predetermined ends. So that, while great designers are commonly equal to themselves, great colorists are much less so. I do not mean to imply that these things are true, without exception, and in every degree, but, commonly, and in some good degree.

For the Valentine, I may say, though to some, it may seem an extravagance, I have never been able to invent the terms that would sufficiently express my admiration of that picture — I mean, of its color; though, as a whole, it is admirable for its composition, for the fewness of the objects admitted, for the simplicity and naturalness of their arrangement. But the charm is in the color of the flesh, of the head, and of the two hands. The subject is, a young woman reading a letter, holding the open letter with both the hands. The art can go no further, nor, as I believe, has it ever gone any further. Some pigments or artifices were unfortunately used, which have caused the surface to crack, and which require the picture now to be looked at, at a further remove than the work, on its own account, needs or requires ; it even demands a nearer approach, in order to be well seen, than these cracks will permit. But these accidental blemishes do not materially interfere with the appreciation and enjoyment of the picture. It has, what I conceive to be, that most rare merit — it has the same universal hue of nature and truth, in both the shadows and the lights which Nature has, but *Art* almost never, and which is the great cross to the artist. The great defect, and the great difficulty, in imitating the hues of flesh, lies in the shadows and the half-shadows. You will often observe, in otherwise excellent works of the most admirable masters, that, the moment their pencil passes to the shadows of the flesh, especially the half-shadows, truth, though not always a certain beauty, forsakes them. The shadows are true in their degree of dark, but false in tone and hue. They are true shadows, but not true flesh. You see the form of a face, neck, arm, hand, in shadow, but not flesh in shade; and, were that portion of the form sundered from its connection with the body, it could never be told, by its color alone, what it was designed to be. Allston's wonderful merit is, (and it was Titian's,) that the hue of life and flesh is the same in the shadows, as in the light. It is not only shadow or dark, but it is flesh in shadow. The shadows of most artists, even very distinguished ones, are green, or brown, or black, or lead color, and have some strong and decided tint other than that of flesh. The difficulty, with most, seems to have been so insuperable, that they cut the knot at a single blow, and surrendered the shadows of the flesh, as an impossibility, to green, or brown, or black. And, in the general imitation of the flesh tints, the greatest artists have apparently abandoned the task in despair, and contented themselves with a correct utterance of form and expression, with well harmonized darks and lights, with little attention to the hues of nature. Such was Carravaggio always, and Guercino often, and all their respective followers. Such was Michael Angelo, and often Raffaelle, though, at other times, the color of Raffaelle is not inferior, in truth and glory, to Titian, greatest of the Venetian colorists; as in his portraits of Leo X., Julius, and some parts of some of his frescoes. But, for the most part, though he had the genius for every thing, for color as well as form, yet one may conjecture he found color, in its greatest excellence, too laborious for the careful elaboration, which can alone produce great results, too costly of time and toil, the sacrifice too great, of the greater to the less. Allston was apparently, never weary of the labor which would add one more tint of truth to the color of a head or a hand, or even, of any object of still life, that entered into any of his compositions. Any eye that looks, can see that it was a most laborious and difficult process by which he secured his results; by no superficial wash of glaring pigments, as in the color of Rubens — whose carnations look as if he had finished the forms at once, the lights and the darks, in solid, opaque colors, and then, with a free and broad brush or sponge, washed in the carmine, lake, and vermilion, to confer the requisite amount of red ; but, on the contrary, wrought out, in solid color, from beginning to end, by a painful and sagacious formation on the pallette, of the very tint by which the effect, the lights, shadows and half-shadows, and the thousand, almost imperceptible, gradations of hue, which bind together the principal masses of light and shade, was to be produced.

For one, I cannot regret what many may regard as the disproportionate labor and attention which he bestowed upon this part of his art. Here, the analogy with the art of writing, again comes in. For certain great effects to be produced upon the reason of mankind, and the condition of the world, you do not desire, nor could you endure, the high coloring of style, or any prettinesses of language. It is only by pure intellect, set forth in the strictest forms of logic, that mankind are to be moved or permanently benefited. Bacon and Locke rule the world of mind; and they do it, not by dainty phraseology, but by compact argument; the closer and severer the better. And even statesmen and orators of the highest order, never toy with language, it is no play with them; but they launch forth their fiery bolts upon an opponent, or a hostile cause, as hot-shot from the batteries of a besieged city; every word, an argument; every argument, a conviction. The more rough, sinewy, the language, and the less of the ornamental, the greater the power. These are the men, not, who please the taste of a few, but who uproot the foundations of current opinion, change the force of philosophies, and shake continents and worlds. For them style is hardly an entity; the word can hardly apply to them. The words they use will not bear adornment, any more than a Bacon or a Newton could wear the costume of a Beau Brummel.

In like manner, the Michael Angelos of art will hardly deign to clothe the Atlantean forms of their Prophets and Apostles in flesh, much less decorate them with color, or any nearer resemblance to humanity. They are gods rather than men. Form alone, colossal form, expressed by strongly contrasted masses of light and shade, (for it can hardly be called color,) is all that such conceptions as those of Michael Angelo, in his Prophets and Sybils, would bear. The splendors of hue, added to such forms, would but detract from the grandeur of the effect.

But there is a class of subjects in which Mr. Allston chiefly delighted, for which color was as essential as form; without which, and without which, in all its attractiveness and most seductive charms, they would be almost destitute of all merit, or could be represented not more truly than by an engraving. I allude to his ideal female heads, and his landscapes. In both these classes of subjects, the objects are few, to the most extreme simplicity, and color constitutes the peculiar charm. Every one must have noticed this, in observing works of art, that the total charm of many a picture, lies, almost wholly, in the exquisiteness of the color. You will find it, not in the drawing, not in grace of form, not in expression, but distinctly and almost solely, in the deliciousness and absolute truth of color. This will be found to be so in the human form, eminently, and even more so in landscape. There is many a landscape, the merit of which lies wholly in the color; its picturesque effect, its power over the imagination, is in the color; in the memories, which it thus awakens, of former scenes and places, even of aspects of the heavens, at night, morning, or sunny noon, of deep woods, or heated, desert plains. An engraving of such scenes would convey no idea whatever, all the forms being poor and meagre, without beauty and without expression. I remember well a picture by the Fleming, Both, of a white cow. The picture was very large; yet, though so large, the only objects were, the cow cooling herself, as she stood in some running water, beneath a spreading tree, — the tower of a church glimmering in the distance over a long sandy reach. But the strength and charm of the picture, lay in the atmospheric hues and haziness of a hot mid-summer day, its aerial perspective, and the general truth of color. Allston's Spanish Girl, and his Italian Scenery, possess these merits, in an eminent degree. These have other merits, as well; but the predominating beauty is in the color. And, is it not exactly so, in scenes of actual nature? The beauty that ravishes the eye is in the color, in the vanishing hues of cloud, atmosphere, and earth; while, at the same time, a distinct or agreeable form can scarce be made out, at all.

I now pass to another characteristic of Mr. Allston's genius, as an artist; I refer to ex-expression.

His power over, and knowledge of, the human countenance was very great, and though, clearly, he is not to be ranked among the greatest artists of this class, he was, nevertheless, to be ranked among those who stood very high in it. But, among those who excelled in this particular respect, I am inclined to think that he cared less than others, to use what power he had; and perhaps, through a dread of caricature, avoided painting an expressive face. In portrait, the difficulty is not in reaching a likeness, but in confining the likeness at the point where decided resemblance is attained and caricature begins. And in historical subjects, in subjects of every kind where sentiment is to be expressed, the same difficulty must occur. It must be comparatively easy to express with strength a strong and decided passion or emotion, — but difficult to restrain the expression within such bounds as to make it effective, yet not offensive. In the numerous works of that class in which he particularly excelled, the ideal female heads, he sought not, but avoided expression, except perhaps, in a single case. The faces are expressionless, passionless, emotionless, like the beautiful head of the Unknown One, in the Pitti Gallery. And certainly, such faces, otherwise well executed, are far more agreeable, or less repulsive, than are sometimes, the extremely pious heads of Guido, and always, those of Carlo Dolce, or Sassoferrato. In the case of these heads by Allston, room is left for the imagination to play and conjure into the features what fancy it may; which is better, where the main object of the picture was of a very different kind. There was manifestly no wish to throw meaning into them, or any meaning to be interpreted by all alike. They were left purposely obscure, of doubtful significancy. There are several in the present exhibition of the Boston Athenæum, of this description, only partly finished, but of the same general character; faces calm, passionless, without sensibility, but at the same time, thoughtful, serious, melancholy, breathing all over, a tender, meditative beauty, which carries in it an indescribable charm, like a twilight scene in nature, where all is divinely beautiful, but all vague, indistinct, indeterminate — the beauty lying in that very trait.

But some, even of his grandest figures, are remarkable for an expression, which, grand and dignified, is yet calm, vague, and hardly susceptible of definition as to the precise sentiment intended to be conveyed. So different, in this respect, from the works of Raffaelle, where, in his greater works, nor only in them, there is not only expression, but a very undoubted expression, with a very unmistakable meaning. Take such a picture as Paul Preaching, or Elymas Struck Blind. Not only the principal actors, but secondaries, and all, without exception, throughout, are marked and strongly marked, by expressions naturally created by the particular incident. This is certainly one of the greatest beauties of those works, and a most decided proof of genius. So also, particularly, with the works of Guercino — full, overflowing with expression, sometimes of a character the most marvellous and subtle. The meanings, which we should say would be the most difficult to convey — almost impossible; half meanings, mixed, double, even these are there; such as pitifulness and reproach, doubt and contempt, and these are conveyed with the utmost precision, with the distinctness and truth of real life. It is not so with Allston; in cases even where it was natural that it should have been so; where there was an open, clear field for a display of all of that kind of power, and where the scene could hardly be expressed at all without a lavish use of it; yet it is not there.

In the great picture of Jeremiah and his Scribe, the expression, for such a subject, is all perhaps that it could be. This figure is altogether of the order of Michael Angelo's Prophets; and, while equalling them in grandeur of form and a divine nobleness in the air, far surpasses them in that gorgeousness of art, which still by no means detracts from any greatness in the effect. But for that which is my only point at present, (I shall speak hereafter of the whole picture,) it seems to me that it utters, as perfectly as one can imagine, the sentiment proper to the subject; the state of mind and feeling of one under the control of a divine inspiration; the air of abstractedness from every present object, of absorption into self, that sudden arrest and pause of every faculty and emotion, while passively the mind receives the divinely communicated truths. All this is finely expressed in the character and fixedness of the countenance, and by the right hand, as if pausing in mid air, while the heavenly message is transmitting. No one can look at this form without being most deeply struck by the air of supernatural dignity spread over the whole figure.

In the form of "Miriam, the Prophetess, the Sister of Aaron," there is well enough expressed, in a finely conceived and well drawn figure, the jubilant air of a Jewish female, singing to the timbrel her song of triumph over the enemies of her country.

"Saul and the Witch of Endor," is more remarkable for the painter's art, which is very high, than for any thing strikingly original or powerful in the expression.

"The Dead Man Restored to Life, by touching the bones of the Prophet." If, in this instance, Allston's power of expression is to be judged by the character of the whole figure of the man in the act of returning to life; or, rather, of life revisiting him slowly, warming the limbs with the flush of health, the eyes heavily opening their lids to the returning light; his genius, in this respect, must be judged

4 *

most favorably, for it is not easy to imagine how either art or the power of conception could be carried further. It appears an absolutely perfect expression of a human form, under the conditions supposed. It is one of those powerful conceptions by which an idea or subject is exhausted, and its demands satisfied. Of the soldiers who surround the mouth of the cave, nothing can be said, but that they express vulgar terror by common-place lines; there appears much monotony in the faces and attitudes.

The work of Mr. Allston, which, as I think, was his most successful one, in point of expression of emotion and state of mind through the countenance, is that which is called the Death of King John. This is an unfinished picture; but, though unfinished in respect to the accessories, the design is determined, the composition complete, and expresses well the whole subject, the forms, and even the costume, roughly indicated with the great masses of light and shade; but the heads of both the principals and the subordinates, with the lines of expression finished, almost to the very final touches; at least, had it lain with me to determine, I should not have dared to allow even the artist himself, to have either added or subtracted a line, or a point of light, shade, or form, so felicitous already, are the countenances of the different groups, in the various shades of their expression. In depicting the scene, Allston followed Shakspeare rather than Hume, in killing the king by poison, administered by a monk, and representing Prince Henry as a full grown man, who was but nine years old; unless, perhaps, by the tall, melancholy figure over the dying king be intended the Bastard of the play, the son of Richard Cœur de Lion, by Lady Faulconbridge. This seems more probable, as it was to him, just returned from France with news for the King, that the Monarch addresses his dying words:

"O cousin, thou art come to set mine eye:
The tackle of my heart is cracked and burned,
And all the shrouds, wherewith my life should sail,
Are turned to one thread, one little hair;
My heart hath one poor string to stay it by,

> Which holds but till thy news be uttered;
> And then all this thou see'st, is but a clod,
> And module of confounded royalty."

The King, as he dies, expresses in the agony of the countenance, some portion, at least, of that inner misery of the heart which could not but torment the conscience of one who had committed every crime, and been guilty of every meanness possible to humanity. But, notwithstanding that all those who are standing by, silent observers of the scene, could hardly have felt otherwise than as all must feel, at witnessing the close of so vile a life, it is a touch of truth and nature in Poet and Painter, that, at that awful moment which swallows up every other feeling, however just and warrantable, in deep commiseration — (the sinner's own horrors of remorse are enough for him) — for themselves, they can only be moved with compassion for the wretch who reviews such a life, and whom such a future awaits; and there is not one face, in all the surrounding groups, that is not marked by lines of the tenderest pity mixed with awe, from the female and the monk bending toward the dying man, up to Prince Henry. All are expressive of the deepest humanity; and from such faces gathered around him, the passing soul could not, at the very last moment, but have caught at a new argument of the mercy of God, from witnessing such expressions of it in the countenances of imperfect, sinful men. If man be thus pitiful, must not God be more so? The whole design of the picture is one of great truth and simplicity; perfectly sets forth the scene ; and, had it been completed, would have redounded largely to the fame of the Artist.

This will close what I have to say of these two characteristics of Mr. Allston, except what may incidentally appear, in criticisms on other parts of the subject. I sum up, as I began, in saying, that, though Mr. Allston is not among the highest in this last named department, he stands very high; but in color, on the highest round of the ladder.

THE LESSER PICTURES.

THE LESSER PICTURES.

Mr. Allston was certainly remarkable for the variety of his powers, and for the variety of departments in which he excelled; and that, not only in the departments of his own particular art, but in other walks of intellectual culture. And within the province of his own special art, he was there marked by variety. A graduate of Cambridge, he enjoyed, of course, all the best advantages which the country affords, of a polite education. He was not only painter, but general scholar as well, and became an author, both in prose and verse. In verse, he reached, by a few efforts, a very general and enviable distinction; in prose, he was confined, not to one department alone, but attained reputation in many.

Metaphysician, novelist, critic, poet, essayist, as he tried all, he was not without much merit in all. In art, he also attempted all its various methods of expressing thought by color and form; and excelled in all he tried, history, portrait, ideal portrait, landscape, marine pictures, cabinet pictures or *genre* pictures, as they are called; in a word, in every thing.

When, a few years ago, the admirers and friends of Mr. Allston collected together, into a single large room, nearly all the pictures by his hand on this side the Atlantic, I suppose that by nothing was one more struck (many indeed, surprised) than by this variety in the departments of his art which he had tried, and in which he had excelled; from the magnificence of the Jeremiah, to the exquisite piece of humor, The Poor Author and the Bookseller, unless it were, perhaps, by the amount of work he had done, notwithstanding the minuteness and carefulness of his finish; and he never dismissed a work from his easel, not only till his employer was satisfied, but till he himself, the most fastidious and difficult of all his employers, was also satisfied.

This various application of his mind to the various departments of his art, while it must have been more agreeable to himself, and gave abundant evidence of that trait of genius termed versatility, and was perhaps, more improving to his own powers than a more limited range would have been, could hardly have served him so well in respect to his ultimate fame, nor, of course, to high excellence in any one department. Art, as he pursued it, was too long for so short a life as the best of us can reach here. One can, for the most part, have time but for a few sketches, and the scene closes—prematurely, to every man actuated by a true ambition, to whatever age he may have reached. Considering the variety of themes to which he was attached and devoted himself, more or less, and he had hardly begun to live at the time of his death. Allston loved the grand and the beautiful with the passion of a mind great in itself and bent on great achievements, in that department. But, almost as well, he loved the humblest work of art, and despised nothing. The quiet Dutch feeling with which he would work upon a stone jar or vase, upon a vessel of gold or silver, or any object of still life, and the perfection to which he would bring it, would hardly have been expected from a mind that preferred and chiefly devoted itself to the sublime and magnificent; to Jeremiahs, Belshazzars, Miriams. Yet that is ever the way with minds of the very highest order. To them nothing is low, which can represent any phase of nature and life with truth. Universality is the attribute of this class of minds. Shakspeare rioted in his Dogberries and Launcelot Gobbos, more, we are apt to think, than in his Hamlets, Othellos, Macbeths; drew them all with equal power and truth certainly, and perhaps enjoyed the work more. And, when you examine the jar or vase in the Jeremiah, or the diamond rings on the fingers of his rich Jews, you see that, in this regard, Shakspeare and Allston were fellows of the same craft.

But one cannot doubt that this versatility of mind and various application of power was, on the whole, injurious to his highest success and his reputation; and for the reason just intimated; — that art is surrounded by so many difficulties that life is not long enough to allow time to climb, one after another, so many of its lofty summits. One, for the most part, must suffice, no matter what the amount of original genius may be; I mean, to attain the greatest excellence in any one. No such man, be he ever so accomplished, can do more than make many brilliant beginnings. It is true that the fundamental principles of the various fine arts, and in all the departments and divisions of each, are common to all, and he who is by nature fitted for one, is fitted for all, and may be capable of excellence in all. But, for the infinite detail of work in each, not perhaps power, but simply, time would be wanting.

There are some branches of art, and indeed, some particular pictures, which demand a very high excellence in many kinds of painting.

History, for instance, requires often not the representing of men, but women also, and various other forms of animal life ; it demands the expression of the passions, in their utmost perfection ; it requires the introduction of landscape, in all its particulars, various kinds of still life and every variety of costume. This is too much for one man to do in one life, and do well ; and he who will attempt it, must fail in many ways. Mr. Allston did, and it was unavoidable. At least, there are but two ways of escape out of the difficulty ; one, that all the less important portions of a picture should be painted with no pretence at perfect finish, in a broad and careless manner, securing only some general good effects ; or all may be turned over to the hands of assistants ; the better way, when possible, and the only conceivable way in which the great artists of the world have been able to accomplish even half the number of works ascribed to them. In such case, the great man made the design and put in the drawing. Subordinates executed all the heavy work of the first coloring, after the drawings, up to a very high degree of finish, and then the master put on the final touches, painting many parts, the heads, perhaps, altogether. Just in painting as it is in sculpture: in Italy a sculptor need never see the marble, but workmen can be found to complete the stone after drawings and models in clay, and in the utmost perfection. Sometimes, the painter artist borrowed the labor of others, in order to expedite works which, alone, it would take him too long to finish, and because, in this way, he could fill the world with much more of the results of his genius, as well as accumulate greater wealth. Sometimes, however, because, in certain departments of the art, he was himself deficient, and was compelled to draw upon the power of another. The figures in the landscapes of Claude were drawn and painted by those whom he employed for that purpose. Giulio Romano was employed by Raffaelle, to paint very large portions of pictures which go under his name. And so of others.

In the case of Mr. Allston, unfortunately,

there could be no help, no assistant, had he desired it ever so much. It must all be done by his own hand, if at all, from the first chalk sketch to the final glaze, — through all the laborious, intermediate stages. One thinks only with a sigh of regret, that the kind of labor which here fell to his lot, could be possibly done by no other hand, — labor, which, though absolutely essential to be done in a very particular manner in order to produce the desired result, yet could, under a little instruction, be readily performed by any person of common ability, under the superintendence of the principal; such, for instance, as the dead or first coloring of his pictures, which, requiring only directions as to the colors to be used in each particular case — an all-important prerequisite — could, for the rest, be done as well by any young tyro, as by an Allston. And so with much else properly belonging to the subordinate and less important work of the artist's studio. Any young student of the art would have been proud of the privilege of placing upon the canvass the first strata of color on which Allston was to place the last; and who would thus have been thoroughly instructed in some of the most valuable secrets and processes by which ultimate effects were to be secured. In this way, had it been permitted, quite a school of young artists might have been put in training, at the same time that he would have been left free to apply himself only to the completing, at the last stages, works, the rough labor of which had been performed by others; and in that way, double, treble the number of his designs would have been completed. But, having adopted the opposite system, of doing all his work with his own hand, he was not, for a great part of the time, so much an artist as a day laborer, performing a drudgery easily to have been thrown off upon others; and accordingly, comparatively few works remain for posterity; very many, considering the amount of work he did himself, and especially, his own fastidiousness and his exalted notions of the character of his art; but few, compared with what might have been done, on a different system, and under which his work would have been, in all respects, equally entitled to the claim of originality.

Another regret one cannot here but feel and express, that it never should have occurred to him, that it would have been an easy thing for him to have collected about him and established quite a school of young artists, whom he would have occupied in the first instance and chiefly, — and it would have been the best instruction he could have given, — in laying the ground-work of his own pictures. Any intimation to that effect, I believe would have drawn to his side an abundance of assistants, whose highest satisfaction would have been the preparation, under his directions, of the first stages of his pictures, and their sole reward, such labors, together with the incidental instructions he could have imparted without loss of strength or time.

The most important instruction to the artist, is that of the purely mechanical processes, — processes which the hints or precepts of a master impart in a few theoretic lessons, or better still, by a few lessons in practice, which are never forgotten, and which save to the young beginner years, perhaps, of fruitless experimenting. Not that any amount of teaching, as I have before hinted, can impart some kinds of knowledge, but that almost any teacher may impart all that is most essential; and, when it proceeds from a master of decided genius, such teaching must bear with it more or less of the impress of the master. Had any such plan been adopted by Mr. Allston, in what a different state would the arts have now been in this vicinity. It might have proved the grand centre of art in the country; a point from which light might have radiated in all directions, where now is almost uncommon darkness. Only the least hint was needed at any time, I am persuaded, to send to his apartments crowds of aspirants ambitious to catch from his presence, his conversation, his art, the spirit of grace, beauty, truth, that overflowed into all the atmosphere about him. And thus, from that luminous centre, one can easily believe, would have originated an American School of Art.

Although however, it be true, that owing to the turn of mind which coveted every form of excellence, he was, perhaps, too various in his labors to reach the loftiest point in any one, yet there was one mental attribute under which almost all his works may be classed, and which stamped itself upon his whole being, which was, grace, beauty. That, as in the case of Raffaelle, was the feeling that overruled all others; the feeling for beauty, in all the widest application of that term. The conception of grandeur was there also; a deep feeling for it, as it is evident, in many of his works, it was his predominating desire to express it, and fill others with the same sublime emotions by which he was himself possessed. But, though it is not to be denied that he in some cases succeeded, it is quite true that he succeeded, not so often, nor to the same extent, in exciting it in the minds of others, as in that of beauty. There he was at home. He dwelt in beauty, and beauty in him. He was it. And in all the works that came from his hand, you see at once the attribute that reigned there ; and how, though defects of one sort and another may be noted, the divine element of beauty is always there. There may be found in his works, at times, a want of expression ; a want of grandeur, where you naturally look for it ; a want of vigor, in conception or execution ; a lack of that abounding life, which, in the works of some artists, draws the spectator like a magnet ; but every where, in all the predominant forms, whether of man or woman, nude or draped, in water, land, cloud, atmosphere, tree or rock ; and, as well in color as in form, beauty and grace are the inspiration, the informing soul ; these, the universal presence that lends attractions and a nameless charm, to every subject that came from his pencil. If it was not every where and in every thing, in every picture, it was always somewhere and in something, and gave its character to the work ; gave that merit which stamped upon it its value. Here he was eminently of the school of Raffaelle and Claude, born under the same star, a vessel of the same divine inspiration.

Mr. Allston had his own peculiar sense of the beautiful, and *that* he endeavored to express; and not any conventional ideas, in which the many agree. Not at all, that he was a man of affectations, or sought rather after the new and eccentric than the true. He was a natural man, a man of simplicity, earnestness and truth, and his object to express with truth, himself and his own conceptions of the beauty, grandeur of nature. But he was very individual; as much so as Correggio or Salvator Rosa. He had his own sense of the beautiful. The face of a woman, for example, is considered beautiful generally, when it is thought symmetrically formed, after the Greek mode perhaps, the features (particularly the nose and mouth) exactly chiselled, as they call it, and a fine vermilion enlivening the skin just there where, according to rule, it should show itself. Such a face, exhibited at the window of a print-shop, would arrest the steps of the crowds who should pass by, and as they passed, the most would exclaim, how beautiful! And it must be so. For there is no fixed standard of the beautiful, but it varies and changes with the individual; and even in the individual, his own standard is apt to change and vary, and differs this year from the last, and to-day from yesterday, just as his general cultivation changes, advances or recedes; or, as suddenly, new sources and impressions are opened to him. That is to say, there are no rules to which to refer, and which can prove this to be beautiful, and that to be the reverse. Each has his own conception of what is beautiful. And though, as I have said, there are certain forms in which the greater part would agree, there are many who would totally dissent; just as we differ in respect to a fragrance. The rose is, to most indeed, agreeable; but not to all, and to some, offensive. And in regard to most other flowers, the differences are infinite. Yet there is a beautiful, as there is a fragrance, but it is created by the mind of the looker-on. That is his beautiful, which he sees to be so, not which others see to be so, or think they can prove such. But, while men in general, and even artists themselves, incline to adopt indolently the conclusions in which others rest, to think their thoughts, and to subscribe to their opinions, I do not think it was the case with Mr. Allston. Especially in the matter under our thoughts, he had his own standard of the beautiful, and expressed it in his own way. In regard to the female head, he certainly differed widely from the common judgment; never representing as beautiful what most would judge to be so. Yet no one can doubt, that to him it was the beauty which captivated and enslaved his imagination, and which he aimed to reveal to others through form and color.

There was no subject, perhaps, of which he was so fond, (and it agreed with the delicacy and refinement of his mind,) and repeated so often, as ideal female heads; not exactly repetitions, of course; but, while all the accidents of the picture varied, the main thought was one and the same ; the type was the same, the individual differences, at the same time, such as to give an air of newness, if not of originality, to each particular subject. It is what would be called an inexpressive countenance, or at most, a ruminating, introspective one ; but, save in a single instance, the Rosalie, really one without expression ; and, in the Rosalie, no expression of joy or grief or melancholy, or any other, so determinate that any two persons would agree as to the meaning intended to be conveyed. The merit of this class of pictures, and it is very great, — they are his greatest works, I suppose, — is that of objects of still life, in a state of such absolute repose, silence, abstractedness, do they live. Life seems almost dead. The Roman Lady, is as if suddenly stiffened into a sort of living death, the very possibility of motion gone, but otherwise beautiful, with the full flush of life and health. Giving up expression, animation, and they are miracles of beauty and grace, — the very perfection of the art of painting. If Leonardo Da Vinci's Mona Lisa, which he was four years in painting, deserved the immortality which has been awarded to it, much more, at least equally, do the Beatrice, the Rosalie, the Valentine. And if the picture of Leonardo's mistress could not be purchased, though covered thick with gold, even deeper should it be piled for the Valentine. In my opinion, there is not existing a picture of this class, which, for the merits of art, stands higher than this. The picture of Leonardo's just named, Raffaelle's Fornarina, of the Tribune, Titian's Flora, all so celebrated; not one possesses in superior perfection, the qualities which make a work of art supremely beautiful, — a transcript absolutely perfect, of the most beautiful nature. This marvellous perfection lies in the color, repose, naturalness, simplicity of the figure. The drawing is all true, the forms all graceful, and the objects of still life, whatever they may be, simple almost to barrenness; yet is the genius lavished upon the color so remarkable, that it must ever remain one of the chief works of the artist, if not his chiefest, scarce ever equalled by any artist of any time, and never surpassed. This may seem an extravagance. But it will not be thought so, if it is considered that this superiority is affirmed, not of the composition, invention, or form, but of the color. All is excellent, and without fault, but it is in the color alone, that this amazing perfection is asserted and claimed; and if it be further considered, that, to this quality of excellence in painting many are almost insensible, many blind, and many incapable of judging, for want, either of a feeling for color, or of cultivation in that particular respect. This is undoubtedly, that element in beauty which requires both a natural eye for color, and also a good deal of cultivation in the way of comparison of one work with another and with nature, to enable one to detect and then feel, the secrets of that beauty that so enchants. Until after a good deal of such comparison and study, but little difference would be discerned between the coarse red and white of a great deal of Stuart's work — with very few though magnificent exceptions — or the glassy, artificial surface of the French and German painters, and that mysterious mingling of hues to produce the very tint of nature, and effect of breathing life, that spreads such an indescribable charm over the Valentine. The lines where grace and comeliness of form reside are comparatively obvious, and almost alike obvious to all, comprehended, moreover, at a glance. Color, on the other hand, in its perfection, is neither seen nor enjoyed at once; its hidden beauty not even guessed. Just as mere style in writing is so often overlooked, and rarely felt in its depths, but by a few who make it a study, so in very many, in respect both to color and style, there is an absolute insensibility; there is the want of a sense of perception, as there is oftentimes, the want of a sense for certain odors, and to poetic beauties.

All the pictures to which I have just referred, and many others, to which I shall presently turn your attention, are examples of that peculiar charm in art, styled by the critics, repose. There is hardly a work from the hand of Allston which is not, either in the whole, or in some considerable part, an instance in point. The word Repose, alone, perhaps with sufficient accuracy, describes the state of mind, and the outward aspect of nature intended by it. It describes the breathless silence and deep rest of a mid-summer day, when not a leaf moves and the shadows fall dark and heavy upon the face of the clear water, which repeats every object near it as in a mirror; the cow on the bank, half-asleep, lazily chewing the cud and flapping away the flies from her side; and the only sound to break the silence, the sleepy drone of the locust; while a warm, misty atmosphere, through which you just catch the roofs of the neighboring village, wraps all things in its purplish folds. Or, it describes the weary foot-traveller sitting upon a stone by the brook-side, as he rests, watching the sheep as they nibble the short grass, or the falling of the autumn leaves, as they alight upon those which had fallen before; these the only sounds, save the gurgling of the water among the pebbles, and the distant Sabbath bell that echoes among the hills. The poets understand this deep repose, and paint no picture oftener.

> " Now fades the glimmering landscape on the sight,
> And all the air a solemn stillness holds,
> Save where the beetle wheels his droning flight,
> And drowsy tinklings lull the distant folds :
> Save that from yonder ivy-mantled tower
> The moping owl does to the moon complain
> Of such as, wandering near her secret bower,
> Molest her ancient solitary reign."

And, in the words of Bryant:

> "For me, I lie
> Languidly in the shade, where the thick turf,
> Yet virgin from the kisses of the sun,
> Retains some freshness, and I woo the wind
> That still delays its coming."

And again,

> " The massy rocks themselves,
> And the old and ponderous trunks of prostrate trees
> That lead from knoll to knoll a causey rude,
> Or bridge the sunken brook, and their dark roots,
> With all their earth upon them, twisting high,
> Breathe fixed tranquillity."

There is much that is closely kindred in the genius of Bryant and Allston. They both love, prefer, the calm, the thoughtful, the contemplative. Their pictures, in color and in verse, paint, oftener than any other theme, this silence, rest, deep repose of nature; the pictures of Allston full of poetry, the poems of Bryant gushing with life and truth.

As in these exquisite lines:

> "And now, when comes the calm mild day, as still such days will come,
> To call the squirrel and the bee from out their winter home;
> When the sound of dropping nuts is heard, though all the trees are still,
> And twinkle in the smoky light the waters of the rill,
> The south wind searches for the flowers whose fragrance late he bore,
> And sighs to find them in the wood and by the stream no more."

Here are music, poetry, and painting — like Canova's Three Graces, embracing each other — bound together in indissoluble union; beautiful apart, beautiful always, but more beautiful when knit together by such a bond.

I may add of this hymn of Bryant, that, like the Elegy of Gray, the one hardly less perfect than the other, the pathos and the beauty are too deep for any one to trust his voice to read aloud.

All the pictures of his ideal women are illustrations of this feeling of repose, this love for the silent, the solitary, the contemplative. The Rosalie, one of the most graceful conceptions that artist was ever able to copy upon canvass, — who shall undertake to guess the thoughts breaking out of that deep, thoughtful eye, the eye of a woman of sensibility and genius, yet for the moment floating in vacancy, or, it may be, arrested by a fancy — she hardly knows what, just as for an instant her exquisite hand is fixed, as she twirls the golden chain that falls from her neck? Of what she thinks, or, whether she thinks at all, it were vain to conjecture. But the art in the picture is almost unsurpassed, even by himself; quite so, save by the Valentine. In her thoughtful repose, sitting with so easy a grace, one is reminded, both in the subject, and the perfection of the design and work, of Correggio's Magdalene, as she lies at length, reading, beneath a tree. The form of the body, so far as it is revealed through the drapery, the rich harmony of the hues that delight without dazzling the eye; the hand so very lady-like, so exquisitely formed, the round delicate fingers so prettily disposed, yet not artificially or affectedly, all this is art so delicious, and of so high a character, that no other among our painters has ever been equal to it, and it fills the mind with pride that in our small circle of new-born aspirants, one even should have arisen capable of achievements that might confer honor upon any age of art, in any land.

In the Roman Lady, as she has been named, very much the same attributes are to be observed. Here, she is not in the state of reverie, but reads from a volume which she holds before her. She is altogether a less attractive person than Rosalie; the face is hard, wooden, unsentimental, and every way less successfully colored, though in all these very respects less faulty than Raffaelle's Fornarina. But if faults may be found with the face, as hard and unattractive, it is not so with the hands, which are eminent examples of the most splendid color imaginable ; both of them in shadow, or half shadow, and are enough to confer celebrity upon any work of art. In both color and drawing, they are specimens of the most perfect art. They actually seem to ray out light, like some of Titian's flesh color, and, as I shall afterwards notice, in the case of the hands of the Jewess in the Belshazzar.

The Beatrice, by most persons, would be thought more beautiful than the Rosalie : but if they differ, they differ only as those things do which are twin in their charms. Both are calm and contemplative, and there is similarity in some points of the costume. Both look out of the picture. There is a national, rather than individual difference, between the two. The calmness of the Beatrice is that of an English, not an Italian lady; so very English, as to deem it unlady-like, if she feels, to express an emotion, in her countenance. The countenance of Rosalie is bursting with emotion not to be restrained; it is as if she might have been the lady-love of Petrarch, Dante, or Tasso, — one who would have watched with enthusiasm, and waited for the maturing fancies of her lover, and as they reached their perfect close, would have thrown a laurel chaplet over his brows in the ardor of her admiration. The English Beatrice would have made no motion.

But perhaps the most exquisite examples of repose, are the Lorenzo and Jessica, and the Spanish Girl. These are works also to which no perfection could be added; from which, without loss, neither touch or tint could be subtracted. We might search through all galleries, the Louvre, or any other, for their equals or rivals, in either conception or execution. I speak of these familiarly, because I suppose you all to be familiar with them. The first named, the Lorenzo and Jessica, is a very small picture, (one of the smallest of Allston's best ones,) but no increase of size could have enlarged its beauty, or in any sense have added to its value. The lovers sit side by side, their hands clasped, at the dim hour of twilight, all the world hushed into silence, not a cloud visible to speck the clear expanse of the darkening sky, as if themselves were the only creatures breathing in life, and they absorbed into each other, while their eyes, turned in the same direction, are bent upon the fading light of the gentle but brilliant planet, as it sinks below the horizon ; the gentle brilliancy, not the setting, the emblem of their mutual loves. As you dwell upon the scene, your only thought is, may this quiet beauty, this delicious calm, never be disturbed, but, may

"The peace of the scene pass into the heart."

In the back-ground, breaking the line of the horizon, but in fine unison with the figures and the character of the atmosphere, are the faint outlines of a villa of Italian architecture, but to whose luxurious halls you can hardly wish the lovers should ever return, so long as they can remain sitting upon that bank. It is all painted in that deep, subdued, but rich tone, in which, except by the strongest light, the forms are scarce to be made out, but to which, to the mind in some moods, a charm is lent surpassing all the glory of the sun.

The Spanish Girl, is another example to the same point. It is one of the most beautiful and perfect of all of Mr. Allston's works. The Spanish Girl gives her name to the picture, but it is one of those misnomers, of which there are many among his works. One who looks at the picture, scarcely ever looks at, certainly cares nothing for the Spanish Girl, and regards her merely as giving a name to the picture ; and when the mind recurs to it afterwards, however many years may have elapsed, while he can recall nothing of the beauty, the grace, or the charms of the Spanish Maiden, the landscape, of which her presence is a mere inferior incident, is never forgotten, but remains forever, as a part of the furniture of the mind. In this part of the picture — the landscape — it must be considered as one of those felicitous works of genius, where, by a few significant tints and touches, there is unveiled a world of beauty. You see the roots of a single hill only, and a remote mountain summit, but you think of Alps and Andes, and the eye presses onwards, till it at last, rests on a low cloud at the horizon. It is a mere snatch of nature, but though only that, every square inch of the surface has its meaning. It carries you back to what your mind imagines, of the warm reddish tints of some of the slopes of the Brown Mountains of Cervantes, where the shepherds and shepherdesses of that pastoral scene passed their happy sunny hours. The same deep feeling of repose is shown in all the half-developed objects of the hill-side, in the dull sleepy tint of the summer air and in the warm motionless haze that wraps sky, land, tree, water and cloud. It is quite wonderful, by how few tints and touches, by what almost shadowy and indistinct forms, a whole world of poetry can be breathed into the soul, and the mind sent rambling off into pastures, fields, boundless deserts of imaginary pleasures, where only is warmth, and sunshine, and rest, where only poets dwell, and beauty wanders abroad with her sweeping train and the realities of the working-day world are for a few moments happily forgotten. This all shows the power of the painter, and yet more, perhaps, of the poet. The only part of the picture that could ever seem a defect to me, was the too formal outline of the small lake, on the bank of which the Spanish Girl sits. And yet one should consider, that it is this very formality, this uniformity, that goes to create in the mind, this feeling of repose, that makes the merit of the whole. The stirring of the water — it is absolutely still — even the rugged indentations of the bank, would have done something to break the charm. I do not remember that the lady possesses any special charms; yet a Spanish girl should, if travellers are to be believed.

The Young Troubadour, is too small to elicit much interest, yet it would not be so if I could consider it equally fortunate in its conception and execution. But it has always seemed to me, that there was a want of adjustment and harmony, which violates the sentiment of repose, which else characterizes it, and disturbs and agitates the observer. And in addition to this, one cannot but think, as in another picture of Mr. Allston's, a Madonna and Child, that he was seduced from his own manner, into a mere imitation of the manner of the old masters, in the forms, and especially, in the tone of color and the handling; it is, as if his aim had been mainly, not to follow the manner of any particular artist, and much less his own, but to copy the manner of all of them, if one may say so, to paint a new picture of to-day, so as, in its thought and its color and general style, to seem like one painted three hundred years ago. At least, I can account for its fashion in no other way so well.

Amy Robsart, — so named, — is not without beauties; but it is, perhaps, one of the least effective of any from his hand.

I turn, with more pleasure, to another work

of Mr. Allston, even though but comparatively few can ever have seen it, but which made upon my own mind, when I saw it immediately after it was completed, an impression of grandeur and beauty, never to be effaced and never recalled without new sentiments of enthusiastic admiration. I refer to his grand landscape of Elijah in the Desert,— a large picture, of perhaps six feet by four. It might have been more appropriately named, "An Asian or Arabian Desert." That is to say, it is a very unfortunate error, to give to either a picture, or a book, a name which raises false expectations. It matters not that you shall find something better than you expected; if it is not that which you expected, because it had been promised, you are at least, disappointed, and in some modes of mind, vexed. Especially is this the case when the name of a picture is a great and imposing one, (as in this instance,) which greatly excites the imagination. What could be more so than this? "Elijah in the Desert, fed by ravens." Yet extreme, and fatal to many, was the disappointment on entering the room, when, looking upon the picture, no Elijah was to be seen; at least, you had to search for him as among the subordinate objects, hidden away among the grotesque roots of an enormous banyan tree; and the Prophet, when found at last, was hardly worth the pains of the search. Sir Walter Scott was always, justly afraid of a name of a book, of any name, that should raise expectation on the part of the public; a proof equally of his genuine modesty, and his practical good sense; so he gave names that meant nothing, Waverley, Guy Mannering, Ivanhoe, The Heart of Mid-Lothian. He observed the same rule in his poems. But, as soon as the intelligent visitor had recovered from this first disappointment, the objects which then immediately filled the eye, taught him that, though he had not found what he had been promised, a Prophet, he had found more than a Prophet, — a landscape, which, in its sublimity, excited the imagination as powerfully as any gigantic form of the Elijah could have done, even though Michael Angelo had drawn it. Nevertheless, all who came in the strictly religious expectation, rather than the artists, who came to find (what they afterwards did find in the Jeremiah) a most real and veritable Prophet, and who knew little and cared less, about art, all such probably, never did recover their equanimity, nor consider the loss less than total.

This landscape is among the few of Mr. Allston's works, which, I suppose, will bear to be classed among the works of sublimity rather than of beauty, or, than among any which illustrate the feeling of repose. Sublime to my mind it certainly was, beyond any picture I have seen since, with the exception of two by Salvator Rosa, in the Guadagni Palace in Florence, the Temptation and the Baptism of Christ. These are great works, worthy of any name and any reputation. They sum up, and even exalt all the peculiar merits of that great artist. Very many of his works fall below his reputation. The greater part do. For he painted in a hurry from a momentary feeling or conception, and his success was, of course, a mere accident. Turner is fabled to work in a somewhat similar way; painting a large picture out of pots of paint which he brings with him, after the canvass is framed and in its place, a day before the Exhibition is to open. But these great works of Salvator betray no marks of immaturity or haste, in either the work or the design. On the other hand, they are grand and magnificent transcripts of that grand and awful nature which haunted his imagination, and of which no truth or reality could possibly be considered an exaggeration. These pictures are both for sale, and could they be brought into the country by any fortunate purchaser, what a foundation would they lay for an Academy of Art! And, if to these, could be added the Elijah of Allston, also probably to be easily had on application, such a gallery, in one department of art, might at once boast an unsurpassed glory. I have said that Allston's picture may be easily had. I will digress so far as to say, that soon after it was completed and exhibited, it was purchased by an English gentleman and removed to England, but fell into disrepute. The story runs, that on occasion of one of our American travellers being abroad and accidentally at the house of the owner of the picture, asking, as was natural enough, to be allowed to see it, the owner (a member of Parliament at the time) could, only with difficulty, be brought to recollect that he had ever possessed such a work, but on doing so at length, a servant was ordered to bring it down from a lumber-room, where it had lain for years, frameless and rolled up among other forgotten rubbish of the same kind. Whether fable or not, if for sale, it would be a great piece of good fortune could it be restored to so many who admire it as a work of genius. It is, however, very likely to be a true story. For the English, in the matter of art, are governed by fashion, solely, not by knowledge, or taste, or sincere relish for it. If Sir Jeremy Fool, R. A., had once set his seal of disapprobation upon it, not all the real merit of this, or any other work, could save it from its fatal doom. There is no individual judgment, that is, in such subjects; prescription is the rule of action. It is not knowledge, genuine connoisseurship, that stamps a picture's worth there, but simply and solely, fashion, money. This is no libel of mine, (if it be one at all,) but you may find it, broadcast, any where on the columns of the London Art Journal, where, on these subjects, the truth is honestly spoken.

But to return to the picture. It is meant to represent, and does perfectly represent, an illimitable desert, a boundless surface of barrenness and desolation, where nature can bring forth nothing but seeds of death, and the only tree there is dead and withered, not a leaf to be seen, nor possible. The only other objects beside the level of the desert, either smooth with sand or rough with ragged rock, are a range of dark mountains on the right, heavy lowering clouds, which overspread and overshadow the whole scene, the roots and widespread branches of an enormous banyan tree, through the tortuous and leafless branches of which, the distant landscape, the hills, rocks, clouds and remote plain, are seen. The roots of this huge tree of the desert, in all directions from the main trunk, rise upwards, descend and root themselves again in the earth, then again rise, again descend into the ground and root themselves, and so on, growing smaller and smaller as the process is repeated, till they disappear in the general level of the plain, or lose themselves among the rocks, like the knots and convolutions of a whole family of huge boa constrictors. The branches, which almost completely fill the upper part of the picture, are done with such truth to general nature, are so admirable in color, so wonderful in the treatment of their perspective, that the eye is soon happily withdrawn from any attention to the roots, among which the Prophet sits, receiving the food with which the ravens, as they float towards him, miraculously supply him.

In this instance, which is rare, Mr. Allston neglected the general truth of nature, to single out and depict a subordinate particular, and that particular having no beauty or charm of its own — though certainly possessing a sort of savage grandeur — simply a piece of natural history and nothing more, which, however excellent in itself, is not the end or aim of this art. We want foliage in a picture, but not a pitch-pine, a locust, a birch, a maple, an oak, or an elm; architecture, but not of stone, stucco, shingle, or brick, nor of one style or another; men and women, but not of one complexion, form, physiological structure or another, of one race or another. There may be such a tree as this of Mr. Allston, with just such roots; but, if there is, none but natives of the country know the fact, or naturalists, whose business it is to be acquainted with it through their science. And, to make it a principal object in a great work of art, is to degrade the art to the rank of a print in Goldsmith's Animated Nature. It was painting a mere whim; the whole tree, roots, branches and all, a mere whim, a *capriccio*. And it only shows how much power was in the artist, that, notwithstanding these essential drawbacks, the total effect was most strikingly that which an original and grand conception could alone produce. You forget the Prophet, the ravens, the roots, and almost the branches, though those were too vast and multitudinous to be overlooked, and were moreover, truly characteristic of the general scene; and dwelt only upon the heavy rolling clouds, the lifeless Desert, the sublime masses of the distant mountains, and the indeterminate, misty outline of the horizon, where heaven and earth become one. The picture was therefore a landscape of a most sublime, impressive character, and not a mere representation of a passage of Scripture history. It would have been a great gain to the work if the Scripture passage could have been painted out, and the Desert only left. But, as it is, it serves as one further illustration of the characteristic of Mr. Allston's art, of which I have already given several examples. For melancholy, dark, and terrific, almost, as are all the features of the scene, a strange calm broods over it all; as of an ocean, now overhung by black, threatening clouds, dead and motionless, but the sure precursors of change and storm. And, over the Desert hang the clouds, which were soon to break and deluge the parched earth, and cover it again with verdure. But, at present, the only motion and life is in the little brook Cherith, as it winds along among the roots of the great tree. The sublime, after all, is better expressed in the calmness, repose, silence, of the Elijah, than in the tempests of Poussin, or Vernet, Wilson, or Salvator Rosa.

THE LARGER PICTURES.

BELSHAZZAR'S FEAST.

THE LARGER PICTURES.

BELSHAZZAR'S FEAST.

If Mr. Allston's mind was drawn, more powerfully than in any other direction, toward beauty and the fit expression of it through his art, he loved, with hardly less devotion, the grand, the sublime, and sought its expression by the same channel. And with almost the like success, did he portray both the one and the other. I say, with almost the like success. For, if there was any difference of power in representing the two emotions, this may have been attributable to the greater frequency with which he treated the one, rather than to any actual difference, either in his power of conception or execution. He succeeded better in the painting of the beautiful, because his mind was more in harmony with it and he therefore painted it more frequently.

That he should, in so many instances, have chosen subjects which involved the sublime, or the grand, may rather surprise us than otherwise, as nature in her outward aspects, so seldom, in the comparison, offers themes which demand its treatment. So also, in representing states of mind, it is seldom that emotions of sublimity are awakened in the mind by any thing we are permitted to know or observe in the character or actions of men, in comparison with what excites within us the love of the beautiful. Nature, externally, is full to overflowing, with sources of the beautiful. You can nowhere turn your eye, above, around, beneath, that your mind is not raised to ecstasy by what you are almost compelled to notice. But it is not so with the other class of emotions. These are but seldom excited, seldom gratified. The sublime must be sought to be found, and is rarely found, though sought. Unless it be maintained, that some of the most common objects of all are, at the same time, the most sublime of which we have any knowledge, or can form any conception, namely, the sun, the moon, the stars, the space that embraces all; our atmosphere, with its infinite changes of cloud and color. And, to a mind that reflects, it is true, that no other objects in nature can compare with them for an inexpressible grandeur; no mountain range of Alps or Andes, no Niagara cataract, no ocean in storm, no African or Asian desert. But then, on the other hand, it is equally true, that custom strips them of their power, and they are as if they were not; that the mind, always seeing them from infancy, in fact, never sees them; and that, in our manhood even, they never become objects of sublimity, except, by an express, and almost painful effort of the imagination. A scientific imagination, the result of the highest knowledge, is essential to the existence of sublime emotions derivable from such objects. To a Newton, or a Herschel, no other object could compare for grandeur, to a single telescopic star, whose distance and size he had calculated, while, to the rest of us, it would necessarily remain but as a spangle on a robe of blue, or a faint twinkle of a firefly.

But Mr. Allston sought the sources of the sublime in almost every case, in states of the human mind, rather than in any outward aspects of nature. He did not overlook the others, but he obviously considered these as affording the more powerful class of subjects; at any rate, it was these that appealed most to his imagination. The Elijah, a mere outward scene, is a grand, sublime landscape; it raises emotions of sublimity in the spectator; and his object was, undoubtedly, to awaken such emotions in all who should look upon it. His object was the same in his large Swiss Landscape, with its vast, angular piles of rock, its deep, still waters, with their clear reflections, the stiff, black pines on the banks, with a solitary pathway, dimly traceable beneath the heavy shadows, along which dark forms are seen stealing their way through the branches. And other works of his could be named, where scenes are depicted, by which emotions are excited which can be aroused only by objects of the very grandest character, as by actual scenes of sublime nature, which show how well he understood, and how deeply he felt, this side of nature. But still, the sources of the moral sublime were those to which he applied for yet higher pleasures, and in which he more frequently sought for subjects for his pencil. The supernatural terror springing from objects obscure and ill-defined; remorse, a tormented conscience, the human being agitated by emotions arising from these and similar sources of woe, afforded subjects for art, which he seemed to think himself capable of treating more effectively still, (though the most difficult of any,) and to which he certainly proved himself entirely equal. The moral condition which he especially delighted in describing, is depicted in the scene of the air-drawn dagger of Macbeth, where a naturally tender, but terrified, imagination makes a fearful reality of a mere phantom of the mind; and this vision of God, as he cannot doubt it to be, revealed to deter him from the deed of blood that he designs, convulses him with terror. He has attempted one scene, taken from a novel of Mrs. Radcliffe, not very unlike the scene from Macbeth, which strikingly shows his power in this department in his art, and to which I shall refer you presently. In the mean time, I first, however call your attention to the Jeremiah, as a principal illustration of the topic in hand. But before doing this, allow me to adduce an instance from Mr. Allston's writings, to show how in unison his mind was with this theme, how readily it received a grand idea and how fitly clothed it in language worthy of the theme. The passage I allude to is in one of his letters, in which he is throwing off easily the thoughts that arise. He is speaking, among other works of art, of a picture of Ludovico Caracci. "I do not," he says, "remember the title of it; but the subject was the body of the Virgin borne for interment by four Apostles. The figures are colossal; the tone, dark and of tremendous depth of color; it seemed, as I looked, as if the ground shook beneath their tread, and the air was darkened by their grief." A sentence worthy of Dante, and exactly in his manner.

I suppose that no better example could be found of Mr. Allston's power of raising the emotions of which we have been speaking, than in the Jeremiah. It is a large picture, eight feet in height perhaps by five in width. It comprises only two figures, the Prophet and his attendant or scribe, Baruch. The Prophet is seated, his head raised, and looking upward with a majestic air. His right arm elevated, the two middle fingers of the hand bent under, the two others erect and pointing upwards. The arm is not, I think, leaning upon any thing, but you receive the idea of a sudden, unconscious arrest of the arm — a suspension of it in mid-air, as if pausing to receive the divine communications; which effect is increased by the singular and awkward position of the two fingers; this very awkwardness showing the state of unconsciousness, in respect to all ordinary impressions; of consciousness, only to the presence of the supernatural. I do not remember the position and action of the left arm. The right foot is thrown out from underneath the drapery, naked, without even sandal, and in its form, its color and whole management, offers one of the finest examples of Mr. Allston's perfect mastery of his art. It is an exhibition, of itself, to any one who loves the art, in its treatment in the most perfect manner, of a very humble, but very difficult object. The other figure, Baruch, is as remarkable for beauty and grace of outline, and splendor of color, as Jeremiah is for massiveness and grandeur. The scribe's subordinate condition is indicated by the deep shadow in which he sits, and the fainter delineation of his whole person. He is placed nearly back to the spectator, and bends over his tablets as in the act of recording the words that fall from the Prophet's lips. It has always seemed to me one of the most faultless of all Mr. Allston's works; and not only faultless, but, with great positiveness, one of the most charming conceptions of his mind. The back-ground of the panel is filled up with the remote architecture of the interior of the Temple. There is to be observed, in this part of the picture, the same perspective power, both in the drawing of the architectural forms, and the management of the light and shade, and of the atmosphere, to produce the illusions of distance, as in the Belshazzar. In the foreground of the picture, stands an immense stone or earthen jar or vase, partly concealed by some heavy folds of drapery, which have fallen upon it, which is worked up altogether with the greatest beauty of effect. To return to the Prophet. This is, perhaps, the grandest form that ever came from Allston's hand; quite certainly the noblest head, with an expression, more nearly approaching the loftiest we can imagine to ourselves, than any other. Indeed it is not easy, even supposing Michael Angelo the artist, to conceive a Prophet or an Apostle of God more completely filling up our ideas of such a Messenger. You feel, the moment you turn your eye upon the picture, that such an one, if any on earth, in the shape of man, is worthy to be the medium of communication between heaven and earth; and, that if he is called *Jeremiah*, he well personates the noblest we can imagine of the sublime old Prophet. And the whole of this grand picture seen together, examined as a whole, reminds one, by the grandeur of the design, by the splendor and harmony of the color, the beauty and grace of the composition of a picture, accounted the second in pictorial merit in the world — the Communion of St. Jerome, by Domenichino. One is made to think of that the more, perhaps, because, like that, it is an upright picture and of about the same size; but more especially, because of its great and surpassing merit in the color, which is the great predominant feature in its magnificent prototype. This merit is especially to be observed in the head of the Prophet, the right hand, and more particularly, in the right foot, beyond which I do not believe art can go, or has ever gone. Then, as a specimen of color, throughout the whole picture, in the drapery, the figures, the background, the still life, yet more in the carnations, this is all no less worthy of admiration. It is also, I will add, an instance to show that the utmost richness and splendor of color, is by no means inconsistent with the most successful treatment of the sublime.

It is many years since I have seen this picture, but I think it not possible that I should have exaggerated any of its merits, and my only apprehension really is, lest I may have failed to do it justice. Those who have not seen it, nor much else of Mr. Allston's work, I am sure, can have very little idea of the superiority of his art; and, in order not to condemn the admirers who have seen it, and that very familiarly, it must be quite necessary that one should make pilgrimages to the shrine of his genius, as we do that of Michael Angelo and Raffaelle. Here I will venture to remark, that there seems to be a fault somewhere, when pictures like this, so calculated to afford pleasure and instruction to so many, particularly to the whole body of our artists, and more especially to the young student, so extremely valuable to them, enough alone, to give an impulse for life, should be hidden away entirely from the eye of the public — not only in private apartments, but in secluded remote villages. The artist is, in that way, defrauded of his just fame, and society of its best means of improvement. I acknowledge the difficulty in the way. That if, in a private dwelling, such a work is freely thrown open, the order of the house is disturbed; carpets are destroyed, and servants and family annoyed. Then, if it is deposited permanently in a public room, the possessor is deprived of pleasures to which he has his right. But, it would be a great favor to the world at large, if such pictures, not possible to be seen in any other way, could be deposited, annually, or occasionally, in a city exhibition-room during three or four months of the travelling season, when very great numbers could be enabled to see them and artists would have an opportunity to examine them and even copy them, if desired.

There are several pictures of Mr. Allston, which are illustrations of the same point now under consideration, his power, namely, over the sublime, but which I have never seen, and therefore could speak of them only by report, namely, Uriel in the Sun, Jacob's Dream, Michael setting the Heavenly Watch at the Gates of Paradise. These, you perceive at once, are subjects grand and sublime in their character, and to be treated in that manner; and the common statements, from the best judges of art relate, that the success of the artist was all you would wish, from the nature of the theme, and all you would expect from the genius of the man. Perhaps, some would be inclined to include the picture of the Raising of the Dead Man by the touch of the Prophet's Bones, in this class; but, remarkable as I think that single figure of the dead man, I should rather regard it as falling into the class of pictures illustrative of the frightful, the appalling, than the moral sublime; in accordance with the definition which Allston himself, in his introductory lecture on Art, gives; denominating the frightful, the horrible, the appalling, as among the sources of the false sublime. The question would of course be, whether this comes legitimately within the limits of this class. For myself, I should be inclined to place it there, and number it as agreeing in character with the Martyrdoms of the Saints, the Flaying of Marsyas, and subjects of that kind. But of this, there would be great difference of opinion.

I now return to a picture already named, "The Bloody Hand," from Mrs. Radcliffe's novel of the Italian. It is rightly considered as belonging to the class we are speaking of. Mr. Allston himself considered it as among his best works. And for a picture of so small size, which seems really unsuitable to a subject designed to awaken the emotions of the sublime, I question if one ever was painted capable of producing impressions of so powerful a character. Emotions of the sublime one can hardly expect to be excited by absolutely miniature objects. If I remember the picture aright, it cannot be more than two and a half feet by eighteen inches, if so much. The subject, is the approach of the Catholic priest

Schedoni, with his attendant, Spalatro, to murder Ellena, the heroine of the novel, and their sudden arrest and horror, at the appearance to Spalatro, among some of the dark passages of an old building, of a bloody hand which beckons to them, and points the way. "Give me the dagger," said Schedoni. Spalatro, instead of obeying, grasped the arm of the confessor, who, looking at him for an explanation of the extraordinary action, was still more surprised to observe the paleness and horror of his countenance. His starting eyes seemed to follow some object along the passage, and Schedoni, who began to partake of his feelings, looked forward to discover what occasioned the dismay, but could not discover any thing to justify it. "What is it you fear?" he said, at length. Spalatro's eyes were still moving in horror. "Do you see nothing?" said he. "I saw it as plainly as I see you; it came before my eyes in a moment and showed itself, distinctly and outspread; it beckoned with that blood-stained finger, and then glided away down the passage, still beckoning, till it was lost in darkness."

The moment seized by the artist is when Schedoni, startled by Spalatro's expressions of terror, pauses, and straining his eyes, tries to penetrate the gloom and see the object of his attendant's alarm; while Spalatro, as in the case of Macbeth, terrified by his tormented conscience, stands stiffened with horror, at the sight of the bloody hand which beckons him the way that he should go. The whole scene is one of supernatural horror, which certainly deserves the epithet of sublime. The figure and expression of Spalatro is very remarkable, expressing a terror by which the very blood is frozen, yet not at all of a common or vulgar type; an expression you would not have thought of but recognise as very nature, the moment you see it; the expression of a horror which nature could endure but for a moment; which drives back the blood upon the heart, or freezes it where it is. The very passage-way where the assassins are arrested, has an air of murder about it; the effect increased by a spade which leans against the stairs. This picture is now in South Carolina.

As my last illustration of this part of my subject, I notice Mr. Allston's large picture, the Belshazzar ; so long begun, so long left unfinished, and so often inquired after during his life ; but, though left unfinished, yet in many parts equal, to say the least, to any thing that ever came from his hand. He had, on the very day of his death, resumed his work upon it ; the paint was yet fresh upon the tints he had last laid on. He was anxious on many accounts, to complete it, and now probably, would soon have done so, had his life been spared but a little longer.

He had met with difficulties in his design, and had found it necessary to re-cast, and re-arrange much that he had thought, at one time, completed. That must often happen, I suppose, in this art. The final effect by no means appears in first sketching, or even in the dead color. It is only the color, and in its full effect, and final touches, that will reveal the real force and character of the design

After all this labor has been fully completed, it is only then that the artist is conscious of errors, sees his mistakes, and at the same moment, learns what a heavy burden of labor is imposed in alterations which are absolutely necessary and unavoidable. Vast labors, therefore, labors never seen, suspected, or known by those who admire the picture in its completed perfection, have to be undergone by the solitary student of art, which have many a time caused the head and the heart to ache and filled the mind almost with despair, ere the original conception can be brought before the eye of the world, in the complete fulfilment of all his ambition. This was a cause of mental anguish, more than once or twice, I have reason to believe, in the instance of Mr. Allston. As soon as he unrolled the picture, on the arrival of the canvass from England, where the picture was begun and almost finished, (as he, at one time, vainly thought,) he sought the judgment of Mr. Stuart, as that of a critic whose knowledge he could trust, and from whose honest severity he had nothing to fear. Mr. Stuart pointed out some, which he deemed fundamental errors. In obedience to his criticisms, the force of which Mr. Allston acknowledged, he went through a series of alterations, connected chiefly with the perspective of the picture, which cost him immense labor, and of the most fatiguing kind; and which a mechanic draftsman could have done equally well, under the least instruction. This single alteration required six weeks of unremitting labor, compelling him to make more than twenty thousand distinct lines in chalk, in circles and segments of circles, in order to bring the whole picture into correct drawing. And this was but the beginning; as all these new drawings were then to be gone over with the ground colors and the final, finishing ones. Any one who knows but little of the art, can but faintly guess what the exhausting, despairing labor was, which all this exacted. And it is not likely that this was the only one, or the last of labors of this kind.

But, had he lived to complete the picture, according to his original design, or even according to his changing purpose, one cannot doubt for a moment, that, through mistakes and alterations, however many and wearisome; through new ideas, and new light constantly breaking in, but always bringing him nearer to the goal, he would at last have worked his way to a successful and brilliant result; a result that would have satisfied himself and exalted still higher his fame, exalted as it then already was. And yet, one may be permitted to express a belief that even such success could hardly have been worth the labors and vexations, the distresses, in short, it cost, nor have been a remuneration for the loss of the many smaller pictures, so much more consonant to his taste and his powers, he would have given to the world in the time that would have been thus rescued had he never attempted the Belshazzar. Still, I cannot accept Stuart's judgment. It was his opinion, given to Dr. Channing, after he had seen the Belshazzar, and with his knowledge of Allston's characteristics, that the picture never would be finished; giving as the reason, "the rapid growth of the artist's mind, so that the work of this month or year was felt to be imperfect the next, under the better knowledge of more time, and must be done over again, or greatly altered, and therefore, could never come to an end." There was a grain of truth in the opinion, but no more. It is ingenious rather than sound, complimentary rather than wise. That Mr. Allston had already completed pictures, large ones too, requiring labor of the severest kinds, and considering his fastidious tastes and the perfection of his finish, completed in an extraordinarily short period of time, is a sufficient refutation of the judgment, without touching the philosophy of the matter.

It might be thought unfair to criticise this picture, as it was left unfinished by the artist. But, as his friends have made it the property of the public, by placing it on permanent exhibition, there can be no impropriety in speaking of it freely; as we are, indeed, bound to do, in the case of every work, in letters or art, from which lessons may be drawn of use to society. They certainly have done right in placing it on exhibition; it is a work too valuable, too beautiful, too much of it near its completion, too instructive in many ways, to have been rolled up forever, or seen only by a few, or hidden from the common eye. And, having thus rightfully been made public, the public, on their part, do right also, in subjecting it to the most thorough examination, and in fully expressing their opinions. Every possible benefit to art should now be drawn from it. The fact that Mr. Allston sought and profited by the opinions of those on whose judgment he could rely, during the progress of the work, makes it sufficiently clear that he regarded it as so far completed, as to make it a proper subject of criticism.

The subject or theme of this picture, styled the Belshazzar, is too well known to need to be stated in the Scripture extracts which describe it. It must be enough to refer to it. A briefer description may, however, be convenient. It is a large picture, painted upon a canvass sixteen feet by twelve. The design of the artist is to represent the effects that would be produced by the appearance of the man's hand coming forth upon the wall in the sight of all, the King, the Court, and all the Magnates of the Kingdom, in the midst of a blaze of supernatural light, and writing on the wall of the palace, the well known words; the effect of all this, and of the interpretation of the words by the Prophet Daniel, upon the multitude of the people there present, upon those sitting at the banquet, and upon the royal persons themselves. The scene which the artist attempted to present, is of a portion of the interior of the Palace of the King, and the architecture belonging to it; the King on his throne; the Queen and her attendants; Daniel and the Astrologers, in the front ground; the Banquet and those who sit at the table, in the middle distance, with the people who crowd a gallery above; then, in the remote distance, the vast interior of an Idol's Temple, with the Idol himself in the centre, beneath a blazing circle of lights; the Temple floor, ascended by successive flights of broad steps, up and down which the people are seen hurrying in their terror. Such, in few words as possible, is a description of the picture.

The first observation I have to offer on the subject is, that the difficulty Mr. Allston experienced during so many years, (more than twenty,) in completing the work, seemed to prove, with sufficient force, that it was of a class of subjects to which his genius was not suited. He was not a man for large pictures, and a multitude of figures. Not that he had not the imagination requisite, not that he wanted any of the intellectual force requisite, — art has seldom, in its whole history, produced a mind of more brilliancy or compass, — but, that he preferred another kind of subject so much, that he undertook any other with reluctance, with too much looking at the amount of labor involved, to be willing to grapple with it, earnestly and heartily, so as to go through it with any higher feeling than that of performing a duty, or doing a job, which could never produce a grand result. Especially, considering the comparative slowness with which he wrought. Yet, they had their attractions, and two he attempted, and others, he sketched. Still, he was not for them, nor they for him. The artist is mirrored in his works. The moral idiosyncrasy shows itself in the picture, the statue, the building, or the book. Mr. Allston was essentially a solitary. In Catholic times, he would have been a monk. He would have been another Angelico, Fra. Bartolomeo, Overbeck. You cannot think of him in public places, mingling promiscuously with men ; you cannot imagine him making dinner speeches, as present at, seeking or enjoying crowds. Yet, a few he sought and loved, and none enjoyed such society more, or adorned it more, just as he instinctively shrunk from the many. What he loved and preferred in life, he did in art. He loved most and excelled most, in single figures. He sought his happiness, and found his success and fame, in the class of ideal forms, — in his Uriel and his Jeremiah; particularly in the female ideal forms, Rosalie, The Spanish Girl, The Valentine, Jessica, Miriam, which especially captivated his imagination. This same inclination for the solitary shows itself in his landscapes, as the Swiss Landscape, and the Elijah.

When, then, he forsook this walk of art for historical pictures of the largest size, it may not so truly be said, as I have already hinted, that he thus grasped what he was not equal to, as that through a momentary fervor, a noble ambition to make real a vast conception that filled his mind and set it on fire, he abandoned a path on which he had long moved with ease and grace, and perplexed himself with themes, which, however attractive to a soaring imagination, were not so much after his whole heart as those of quite another kind. Moreover, he was not, now, expressing or uttering himself, as before, but rather treating a subject. *He* was in the Valentine, the Rosalie, the Jessica; the man was in them. He could feel little sympathy with the crowds he was obliged to paint in the Belshazzar, (or only here and there one,) and must have tired of them. So with the architecture, of which there is a great deal; so too, with the brazen and golden vessels, the king's throne, costumes, and other objects of still life; — they cost infinite labor, and he worked them up, as far as he went, in the spirit of Gerard Dow, and though he was not disinclined to work of that sort, there was too much of it, the labor and time demanded were too much. He must have felt it as a waste. He was not the person, moreover, with his slight frame and little strength, to go mounting up ladders, and working on stagings, and using brushes large as a house painter's. It is really painful to think of Allston laying on the priming coats of a picture like the Belshazzar. Pupils should have done all that work after the drawing had been made. And even when he came to the finishing, it became only so much the more laborious, and that was work which none but he could do. For every minute touch, with his taste, his eye and feeling, which penetrated to, and was satisfied with only the whole and exact truth, he must have found it necessary to descend his ladder, retreat to the proper point of sight, to learn the precise effect of the little point of light or shade, or color he had added, then remount to his position; and repeat the process, day after day, month after month, during the killing heats of summer, and the killing frosts of winter. I can conceive of nothing more painfully toilsome, to a man of a feeble constitution. No doubt, long use would enable an artist to paint on this large scale, as easily as on any other, calculating for the force of color at a great distance, and doing the work as another would a cabinet picture close to his eye, but it could be only use, that could enable one to do it; and, in the case of the only work of this character, the difficulty must have been all but insurmountable.

A man does not succeed quickly or well, in any hing he does or attempts against the grain, however he may ultimately fight his way to it, after a fashion. I think that to have been the case with Mr. Allston. He felt that he was out of his true path, and that, after all, he might meet with but partial success, not enough to satisfy his aspirations. By such convictions I believe he was often disheartened and threw off the task in a sort of despair; and mean time, soothed and delighted himself in some Lorenzo and Jessica. This, I believe to be the true account of the non-completion of this large picture, for so many years. Add to this, there was evidently a dissatisfaction, on his own part, with the design; not, perhaps, with the very principal features of it, but with very important parts, and which led to many great and laborious changes. The subject was seized only partially. He did not see the whole at once, all the diverse parts in their proper relations to each other. It was not one of those felicitous conceptions, which belong only to minds of the very highest order, minds of a universal sweep, by which a subject is seen, almost as a divine intelligence would see it, where every thing is as if it could not be imagined to have been different, as in the designs of Raffaelle. He was ever altering, nor at the last, had he apparently reached the final limit of change. It has been stated that the appearance of Martin's remarkable work on the same subject, was a reason why he abandoned it; that Martin had drawn from him the most original feature of the picture, the proceeding of the light from the miraculous letters of the inscription. What the truth of this was, I do not know. Only it seems far more likely, that the causes just named were the more real ones that arrested his hand so long.

It is true that he had, once before, in the time of his youthful vigor, attempted, and in a very brief period, completed a great historical work, of a very large size — "The Raising of the Dead Man by the touch of the Prophet's Bones" — a picture which, with some faults, could never have been designed or executed by any but a person of very remarkable powers. Indeed, Mr. Allston never manifested more power than in some parts of this work. But it was too much confined to the single figure of the reviving dead man. Still, whatever defects or faults are to be noted, they are all abundantly atoned for by the genius that blazes forth in the wonderful figure of the dead man, whom, at the touch of the Prophet's bones, you see slowly raise himself, a dead body just deposited in the tomb, yet beginning to move, the faint flush of returning life tinging the lips and the cheeks; the eyes, though heavily unclosing, still glazed and dead; a fearful object, and only too true to our imaginations. As I have before aimed to show, it is a picture that comes under Mr. Allston's own classification of the appalling, rather than the moral sublime. It was a great, difficult, complicated work, and called for high powers and vast labor.

But the Belshazzar was a vastly more formidable undertaking, and if the subject just described was one from its nature little suited to his mind, much less was this. This calls for all the most difficult departments of the art, makes the highest demand upon the mind in the conception of the subject, and its management in the composition, and again the highest demand for the artistic powers absolutely required, for even a tolerably successful treatment of it. The subject is one of the truest sublimity; the miraculous interference of the Deity, by a Prophet, to declare the speedy overthrow of a great and prosperous kingdom, in the letters of fire emblazoned upon the wall; crowds of the great men of the empire in their appropriate costumes, as far as the study of antiquity could supply them; the awful Prophet interpreting the judgment of God; the terror and consternation of an agitated populace; the magnificence of a royal entertainment, with its gorgeous array of gold and silver vessels; the King upon his throne, in a state of terror which caused the joints of the knees to loosen; the Queen, with her attendants and the royal concubines; the Priests and the Astrologers, equally humbled and enraged at the success of the Jew, in interpreting the writing, which they had failed to do — here were difficulties enough to appal the stoutest heart, and almost daunt the loftiest courage, laying a peremptory claim on every power that could belong to the most gifted genius. It would be no shame to confess a failure where none but powers, almost more than man's, could succeed; which asked for a sublime Poet, not less than a sublime Artist. But this, while it held out so brilliant a reward to complete success, was enough to break the spirit beneath the intolerable burden of an unavoidable apprehension. And I cannot doubt that it was a cause of no little mental suffering.

I shall now go on to specify two faults, which I think would strike any one in examining this picture; in the want of expression of character, and in the architecture.

There is a want of power in the expression of the various passions, emotions, feelings which properly belong to the subject, or rather, constitute it; without which, or with which, erroneously or feebly expressed, such a picture must fail, or would scarcely be said to exist. Not, of course, that Mr. Allston has not shown, abundantly even, great power to express passion, feeling, through the language of the countenance; but, after all, as I have already mentioned at some length, it is a limited power, not universal, and does not satisfy the demand made by a work of this high character. I do not say that it might not have become all we could desire, had he lived, but it is not so now, where the picture seems completed. But generally, I have said, his power seems limited on the one hand, to an expression of the stronger, more intense emotions, as fear, terror, malignity; and on the other, to emotions so vague and shadowy, as to leave it doubtful what was the feeling or state of mind intended to be conveyed, or whether any at all, or of a character so definite as to be capable of being conveyed by art. For those most delicate, subtle, but yet most precise shades of meaning, often quite complicated, yet still attended by no uncertainty as to their sense—the highest intellectual achievement in art — to be seen in so many of the works of Raffaelle and Guercino, these are not found in Mr. Allston; not in such perfection as to be a characteristic. In the work before us, the grosser sentiments of terror and malignant hatred, are not very successfully treated. That difficult line is overstepped which divides a strongly expressed sentiment from caricature. This is obvious in the Astrologers, with one exception, yet, we may feel quite sure that those heads would have undergone great modification.

In regard to the King, the artist appears to have been governed by a determination to avoid caricature of the sentiment of terror, but, avoiding that, he did not succeed in substituting any other in its place that could be considered as successful. The intention seemed to have been, to exhibit a person under the influence of a fear and awe so extreme as to cramp and convulse the form, freeze, stiffen it into a mere rigid, lifeless clod — an almost impossible feat to perform in art, and certainly, not successful here — though here, it must be said, that the figure, as it is now seen, had been painted over by Mr. Allston, as if dissatisfied with it, and since his death, restored in a good degree. Apparently, with his conception and execution of the Queen he was satisfied, and the form seems perfectly finished, in a costume to the last degree magnificent; gorgeous in its ornament, yet in perfect taste. The face, a very noble one; but the expression, while strong, not such as you would look for, nor natural to the scene; for it is of scorn and contempt, rather than of awe or terror. The firm grasp with which she seizes and holds the hand of one of her attendants, seems to confess the need of support and help; but, setting this aside, and she is too proud of heart, though in the midst of so dreadful a scene, to express in her countenance any thing save utter scorn and contempt for what she holds to be the mere juggler tricks of cheating priests. If the King sinks down in dismay, she will stand up against the worst that may happen. In all her bearing, she is every inch a Queen. And her presence alone, with her queenly beauty, her regal pride, her womanly grace, as she bends her dark eye on the Prophet, is enough to spread a glory over the whole scene. She is the only person with whom the spectator sympathizes. The Prophet Daniel fails of any good effect; the figure wants not only expression but force; the form is good, but both head and face want grandeur and power. The story used to run, that the great Daniel of to-day was to be represented in the Prophet. But there was no so good fortune in store for us.

A great proportion of the other figures are without expression of one kind or another. Those at the Banquet appear to be in a state of commotion; some terrified, some apparently fainting, but more express no emotion of any kind, which seems unaccountable in the midst of so dreadful a scene; those upon the steps of the Idol's Temple are flying in different ways, as if not knowing which way to turn; those in the gallery above the tables, are in the same mixed state, some agitated, but more unconcerned spectators of what one might suppose could be witnessed by none with indifference, and by most, only with extreme terror or a religious awe, by which even pagans must be affected, as they must have seen at once, that the apparition was beyond the arts of their Magicians. A group of five or six, near the centre of the picture, is every way very remarkable for a display of the Artist's power in costume, drawing and color. They may be supposed to be Jews. Some are seated. None, apparently, concerned in what is going on. One is in a state of wonder, or some such emotion; the rest, without any expression whatever. It is true that some time must have elapsed since the first coming forth of the Hand; for the King had first sent for the Astrologers, who arriving, and after consultation, failing to give an interpretation, the Queen had then come in and advised the sending for Daniel. He had been sent for, had entered the hall, and had interpreted the writing. All this implies the passage of considerable time, and the lapse of time would naturally lead to a gradual subsiding of the first tumult of surprise and horror, yet, at the same time, shows that at that very precise moment, selected for the central point of time of the picture, when the Prophet utters the word "UPHARSIN," "Thy kingdom shall be taken from thee," there would be almost more than a renewal of the horror and excitement on the first appearance of the handwriting, on the part of the Babylonians and the King; and on the countenances of the Jews, either the deepest awe at the miracle of their God, or otherwise, triumphant glances, or shouts of joy at the predicted overthrow of the kingdom of their ancient enemy. They could not have kept their seats, motionless and apathetic, while such scenes were transacting. I can readily understand that Mr. Allston must have wished to avoid a mere vulgar expression of theatrical horror, such as we observe in Martin, whose main object was not to express character in its finer shades, but to produce all the effect he designed by startling contrasts of light and shade, and especially by architectural perspective. But, while he certainly avoided that, he fell into an opposite extreme, of presenting too many persons, (principal ones too,) figures and faces, without any meaning at all; for the very primal object of such a picture, when the forms are of the size of life, must have been to express the character and sentiment proper to the scene; by which the whole occurrence could be fitly represented, and, if such character and sentiment are not expressed, no other merits of any kind, can atone for the loss. In the great masters of the art, for example, Raffaelle, it is, at least very often the case, that in a picture where there are many actors in the scene, of various ranks and conditions, though all do not utter a common expression variously modified, the effect of which would be monotonous; all express something, and with great preciseness, not necessarily having respect to the main thought of the picture, but to many things quite different and remote from it; we find many groups, each with its own subordinate interest. This lends great variety and life to the whole work. This is Shakspeare like, and like nature.

Bring numbers, a crowd together any where, and though by no means will all be, immediately, or alike, or deeply interested in the common object which brought them together, yet all will be interested about something; and a thousand by-plays and by-scenes will be transacting, — all sorts of things, the most incongruous, will be soon going on.

Another defect in this great picture, of a different kind, but very great and obvious, is to be seen in the treatment of the architecture, which constitutes a very prominent part of the scene. It is, quite obviously, a portion of the picture in an unfinished state. But no kind of finishing could have essentially changed its character, or removed the objections which exist to it; as the difficulty lies, not in the details, but in the very forms and proportions themselves; in the very force of the color which is requisite to express the forms as they must be, to be in proper relation to the other objects of the scene. The final glazings may have done something to relieve the difficulty, throwing it a little more out of sight, but could not have removed it. The fault is in the effect of littleness, meanness, produced by the rows of small columns in the front of the picture, of not more than some ten or twelve feet in height, looking like the pillars of a country meeting-house gallery. Such columns are wholly out of place in any royal hall or palace; especially so, in any Babylonian, Assyrian, Egyptian architecture, and utterly inadmissible where ideas of grandeur, sublimity, are the emotions sought to be raised. As a work of art with such an intent, these columns blast, blight and kill the whole conception. It is an irredeemable blot; a fatal blemish. Ever so many trivial forms can never make one grand or sublime one. You may plant columns, or arches, all over the Roman Campagna, running from the gate of the city to the opposite Apennines, but, if they be but some ten or twenty feet in height, they will only seem the smaller and meaner for their number; they will only be posts, not columns. The great Cathedral of Pisa has perhaps three or four hundred columns in the interior, but, being very small, there is no effect of grandeur produced; it only looks like a large plaything, and the pillars like turned sticks. So in this picture. Here, the columns are but few, which is better; but, if one might be so bold, they should all be swept away and if any thing of the same sort in their place, the dim outlines only, of two or three vast pillars, reaching upward into a gloomy undefined height, where the forms are lost. The obscure, the unbounded are elements of the sublime, never the clear, and sharply defined.

I can feel no misgiving about the justice of this criticism. But, the defect which is so obvious here, is not to be observed, but a principle the very contrary carried out and with the greatest majesty of design and effect, in the interior of the Idol's Temple, which fills up all the back-ground of the picture. In the remote parts of the picture, in the boundless interior of the Temple, it is treated in a manner truly grand, and the wonder of wonders is, how the same principle could have been so mistakenly treated, in another part of the same work. The management of the architectural forms in the Idol's Temple, is one of the grandest features in the whole work. There, there is sublimity, indeed; where are seen columns of Egyptian size and proportion, towering upward till lost to sight; the dim atmosphere of the vast chamber, the countless flights of steps, up which the crowds are hurrying and then spreading over the floors, the mysterious form of the brazen God, with the circles of blazing light above; these all conspire to fill and excite the mind in the highest degree, and prove the great power of the artist. The perspective there, both in the form, the lines of the architecture, and especially, in the atmosphere, is a perfect triumph in that branch of the art. Had the whole been completed in that spirit and power, even Martin's picture, in that feature in which it has most, or any merit, would not have exceeded, if it had equalled it.

But the great charm of the picture is where Mr. Allston always charms, in the color; so far as completed, nothing, to our eyes, remains to be added. It is the color of the great Venetians; rich, gorgeous, yet chaste, pure, and harmonious. Had it enjoyed the happy fortune to have been finished up to the Artist's conceptions, it would have been a picture, which, for particular merit, would have gone near to eclipse all that had gone before it, of which, at least, we have any knowledge. For, though Paul Veronese may have left more grand and fruitful inventions, and stamped his works with a luxuriousness of fancy to which there is nothing like, and though his color, also, was admirable every way, yet he never worked up any one of his pictures, I imagine, to that minuteness and perfection of finish so striking in this; which, though so large, completed, would have had at once, all the truth and delicacy of a cabinet gem and the breadth and grandeur which belong to colossal subjects; which is just the truth of Nature, whose works, though ever so large, are never finished with any the less minuteness and perfection. The two traits are compatible and consistent, though Art so often disjoins them. For the finest example of color, in any part of the picture, I should refer you to the group of the Jews, in the centre; all in shadow, but all finished to such perfection, that not perhaps a single touch more would have been needed. Let the group be carefully examined under the strongest light that can be thrown upon it, it will bear it all, and it requires it all, — the more concentrated and powerful, the better you will see, and the more objects and forms, otherwise invisible, will come into view and add to the effect of the whole. Nothing is slurred over, all is done with equal fidelity; objects in shadow, as objects in light; and it is in objects in shadow done with this equal perfection, that the greatest beauties are to be found in paintings. Many, ignorant of this, overlook the best portions of a picture, observing with any attention, only what is forced upon the sight by the strongest light. For beauties in shadow, I would refer particularly to the same group, and to the hands of the Jewess, stretched out, as she bends down, expressive of religious reverence toward God or to his Prophet, close to whom she sits, where you will see painting in the forms, color, perspective of the palm and fingers, that never was surpassed; for the color, it really seems self-luminous, and rays out light, as it were, into the dark all around, an effect I never saw elsewhere, save in Titian and the Elder Palma. There are other particular points of excellence in color worth noting, particularly the head of one of the Astrologers, who stands fronting the spectator, (which is not more remarkable for its color, grand as Rembrandt's, than for the successful expression of the deepest malignity); the Queen, the head of Daniel, a servant at the tables, just beyond the kneeling Jewess, and I must add, the brazen and golden vessels, and the gems that glitter on the fingers of many—this is all admirable work. Of the great art shown in the color of the great Hall, and in the Idol's Temple, I have spoken. But beyond all this excellence, in particular parts of the picture, there is a much higher one shown in the tone of color and harmony which pervades the whole, which is all as if painted from a single palette and at one sitting, so exquisitely are the hues, the lights and the darks, balanced and blended. The idea of contrivance, in truth, does not suggest itself; it seems one grand work, not of Art, but of Nature, where all must be true and right. The color affects you in the same way. All this merit so palpable, though the work can only be said to be partly finished. This fills one with highest admiration, and at the same time, saddens him with melancholy regrets, that so noble a conception, which, had life been spared, we are confident would have been completed in the same spirit of power in which it had been commenced and prosecuted, should have been arrested midway. The effect of the whole, upon an appreciating mind, is that of an exquisite piece of music, like the intricate, but ever harmonious movements of Beethoven's Symphonies, or the melting, blending strains of an Æolian harp.

In closing these Lectures, I am ready to

acknowledge, no one more so, that I have not been able to satisfy myself in representing Mr. Allston's mind and art. I have been obliged to omit much which I wished to say, as I have said much, doubtless, that were better left unsaid. But such fault is incidental to all writing for temporary and public purposes. They can only be regretted; not apologized for.

But I am quite inclined to offer an apology to you, who have listened to me, to myself, and to the venerable shade of the great Artist of whom I have discoursed, to whom I have tried to do all honor, and who now perhaps, with Virgil and Dante, congenial souls, with Michael Angelo and Raffaelle, also congenial souls, but not more so, wanders by the bank of some clear stream, beneath grateful shades in the Elysium for which we all sigh, for venturing as I have done, so many observations on the last unfinished work of the author — especially for such as may seem to have borne on the face any blame. I declare it is with feelings of severe self-reproach that I recall what I have written of blame, so sure am I that with time, he would have brought the work to a perfect close. But, when I have at any moment uttered such phrase, I believe I have coupled with it the extenuating clause, that there was no fault that might not be amended; and I repeat now emphatically the conviction, and it is only what is due, that, from what we know of Mr. Allston and his mind, of his spirit of patient perseverance, his love of perfection, and search after it in all he attempted, it is quite certain, that had he lived, he would have surmounted every difficulty, triumphed over all obstacles, and brought his labor to a perfect and brilliant close. It were unphilosophical to think otherwise. I am clear in the belief ——

NOTES.

THE following is the Catalogue of Mr. Allston's Pictures, exhibited at Harding's Gallery in Boston, in the year 1839, and referred to on Page 50.

No. 1. — Date 1813.

THE DEAD MAN RESTORED TO LIFE, BY TOUCHING THE BONES OF THE PROPHET ELISHA.

"And the bands of the Moabites invaded the land at the coming in of the year. And it came to pass as they were burying a man, that behold, they spied a band of men, and they cast the man into the Sepulchre of Elisha; and when the man was let down, and touched the bones of Elisha, he revived." — 2 Kings, chap. xiii. v. 20, 21.

ACADEMY OF FINE ARTS, Philadelphia.

No. 2.

JEREMIAH DICTATING HIS PROPHECY OF THE DESTRUCTION OF JERUSALEM TO BARUCH, THE SCRIBE.

Vide Jer. Ch. xxxvi. MISS GIBBS, Boston.

No. 3.

THE TRIUMPHAL SONG OF MIRIAM ON THE DESTRUCTION OF PHARAOH AND HIS HOST IN THE RED SEA.

"Sing ye to the Lord, for he hath triumphed gloriously; the horse and his rider hath he thrown into the sea." — Exodus, Ch. xv.

David Sears, Boston.

No. 4.

THE WITCH OF ENDOR RAISING THE SPIRIT OF SAMUEL BEFORE SAUL.

Vide 1 Samuel, Ch. xxviii. Col. Perkins, Boston.

No. 5.

THE FLIGHT OF FLORIMEL.

Vide Spenser's Faery Queen. James F. Baldwin, Boston.

No. 6.

POLYPHEMUS IMMEDIATELY AFTER HIS EYE WAS PUT OUT, GROPING ABOUT HIS CAVERN FOR THE COMPANIONS OF ULYSSES.

Drawn on ship-board. James F. Baldwin, Boston.

No. 7. — 1805.

SWISS SCENERY.

Isaac P. Davis, Boston.

No. 8.

A MOTHER WATCHING HER SLEEPING CHILD.

JAMES McMURTRIE, Philadelphia.

No. 9.

EDWIN.

Vide Beattie's Minstrel. ROBERT GILMOR, Baltimore.

No. 10.

BEATRICE.

SAMUEL A. ELIOT, Boston.

No. 11.

ITALIAN SCENERY.

SAMUEL A. ELIOT, Boston.

No. 12.

THE VALENTINE.

GEORGE TICKNOR, Boston.

No. 13. — 1810.

LANDSCAPE. ITALY.

EDMUND DWIGHT, Boston.

No. 14.

AMERICAN SCENERY.

Time, afternoon, with a south-west haze. EDMUND DWIGHT, Boston.

No. 15.

A ROMAN LADY.

Edmund Dwight, Boston.

No. 16.

LANDSCAPE.

Warren Dutton, Boston.

No. 17.

THE EVENING HYMN.

Warren Dutton, Boston.

No. 18.

LANDSCAPE.

Time, after sunset. Charles Codman, Boston.

No. 19.

ISAAC OF YORK.

Vide Ivanhoe. The Athenæum, Boston.

No. 20.

SKETCH OF A POLISH JEW.

The Athenæum, Boston.

No. 21.

PORTRAIT OF BENJAMIN WEST, Late President of the Royal Academy, London.

The head painted in London, 1814, the drapery and background added in 1837, Cambridge.

The Athenæum, Boston.

No. 22.

AN ITALIAN SHEPHERD BOY.

ROBERT C. HOOPER, Boston,

No. 23. — 1805.

PORTRAIT OF THE ARTIST.

Painted in Rome. NATHANIEL AMORY, Newport.

No. 24.

MOONLIGHT.

DR. BIGELOW, Boston.

No. 25.

LANDSCAPE.

POWELL MASON, Boston.

No. 26.

HEAD OF ST. PETER.

A study for the large picture afterwards painted for Sir George Beaumont, now in a Church at Ashby de la Zouch, England.

GEORGE BANCROFT, Boston.

No. 27. — 1811.

COAST SCENE ON THE MEDITERRANEAN.

T. WILLIAMS, Boston.

No. 28.

A SKETCH OF A POLISH JEW.

J. S. COPLEY GREENE, Boston.

No. 29.

A SKETCH OF A POLISH JEW.

Thomas Dwight, Boston.

No. 30. — 1811.

A POOR AUTHOR AND A RICH BOOKSELLER.

T. H. Perkins, Jr., Boston.

No. 31.

LANDSCAPE.

Rev. Dr. Lowell, Boston.

No. 32. — 1804.

RISING OF A THUNDER-STORM AT SEA. PILOT BOAT GOING OFF TO A SHIP.

S. D. Parker, Boston.

No. 33.

DONNA MENCIA IN THE ROBBER'S CAVERN.

Col. William Drayton, of South Carolina — Philadelphia.

No. 34.

PORTRAIT OF SAMUEL WILLIAMS, Esq.

Timothy Williams, Boston.

No. 35.

ROSALIE.

Nathan Appleton, Boston.

No. 36. — 1810.

LANDSCAPE.

Isaac P. Davis, Boston.

No. 37.

THE TUSCAN GIRL.

David Sears, Boston.

No. 38.

JESSICA AND LORENZO.

Patrick T. Jackson, Boston.

No. 39.

THE SISTERS.

Francis Alexander, Boston.

No. 40.

THE YOUNG TROUBADOUR.

Vide Allston's "Lectures on Art and Poems," pp. 340, 341.
J. Bryant, Jr., Boston.

No. 41. — 1806.

FALSTAFF AND HIS RECRUITS AT JUSTICE SHALLOW'S.

William Sullivan, Boston.

No. 42. — 1811.

PORTRAIT OF THE LATE Mrs. WM. CHANNING.

Rev. Dr. Channing, Boston.

No. 43. — 1799.

LANDSCAPE.

Painted when at College, Cambridge.

General Sumner.

No. 44. — 1799.

LANDSCAPE.

In possession of the Artist.

Painted when at College, Cambridge.

N. B. These youthful efforts are exhibited as objects of curiosity.

No. 45.

STORM AT SEA.

The ship Galen, in which the Artist returned from Europe. Drawn on ship-board.

Col. Perkins, Boston.

THE ROSALIE. Page 72. The following verses by the Poet-Artist give us his own description of the Rosalie.

"O, pour upon my soul again
That sad, unearthly strain,
That seems from other worlds to plain;
Thus falling, falling from afar,
As if some melancholy star
Had mingled with her light her sighs,
And dropped them from the skies!

"No, — never came from aught below
This melody of woe,
That makes my heart to overflow,
As from a thousand gushing springs,
Unknown before ; that with it brings
This nameless light, — if light it be, —
That veils the world I see.

"For all I see around me wears
The hue of other spheres ;
And something blent of smiles and tears
Comes from the very air I breathe.
O, nothing, sure, the stars beneath
Can mould a sadness like to this, —
So like angelic bliss."

So, at that dreamy hour of day
When the last lingering ray
Stops on the highest cloud to play, —
So thought the gentle Rosalie,
As on her maiden reverie
First fell the strain of him who stole
In music to her soul

THE SPANISH MAID. Page 77. Mr. Allston accompanied the first exhibition of this picture with the following ballad.

Five weary months sweet Inez numbered
From that unfading, bitter day
When last she heard the trumpet bray
That called her Isidore away, —
That never to her heart has slumbered.

She hears it now, and sees, far bending
Along the mountain's misty side,
His plumèd troop, that, waving wide,
Seems like a rippling, feathery tide,
Now bright, now with the dim shore blending.

She hears the cannon's deadly rattle, —
And fancy hurries on to strife,
And hears the drum and screaming fife
Mix with the last sad cry of life.
O, should he, — should he fall in battle!

Yet still his name would live in story,
And every gallant bard in Spain
Would fight his battles o'er again.
And would she not for such a strain
Resign him to her country's glory?

Thus Inez thought, and plucked the flower
  That grew upon the very bank
  Where first her ear bewildered drank
  The plighted vow, — where last she sank
In that too bitter parting hour.

But now the sun is westward sinking;
  And soon, amid the purple haze
  That showers from his slanting rays,
  A thousand Loves there meet her gaze,
To change her high, heroic thinking.

Then Hope, with all its crowding fancies,
  Before her flits and fills the air;
  And, decked in Victory's glorious gear,
  In vision Isidore is there.
Then how her heart 'mid sadness dances!

Yet little thought she, thus forestalling
  The coming joy, that in that hour
  The Future, like the colored shower
  That seems to arch the ocean o'er,
Was in the living Present falling.

The foe is slain. His sable charger,
  All flecked with foam, comes bounding on.
  The wild Morena rings anon;

And on its brow the gallant Don
And gallant steed grow larger, larger;

And now he nears the mountain-hollow;
The flowery bank and little lake
Now on his startled vision break, —
And Inez there. — He's not awake!
Yet how he'll love this dream to-morrow!

But no, — he surely is not dreaming.
Another minute makes it clear.
A scream, a rush, a burning tear
From Inez' cheek, dispel the fear
That bliss like his is only seeming.

Globe Man's Daily Story

Salesmanship knows no bounds.

A nearby tailor was in the act of selling his best friend a new suit. He was raving about the garment.

"I'm telling you, Harry," the proprietor said, "that even your best friend won't recognize you in that suit! Just take a walk outside for a minute and get the feel of the garment."

Harry went out and returned a moment later. The proprietor rushed up to him with a happy smile.

"Good morning, stranger," he beamed. "What can I do for you?"